REFERENCE

HOW TO IDENTIFY AND COLLECT AMERICAN FIRST EDITIONS

A GUIDE BOOK

Jack Tannen

ARCO PUBLISHING COMPANY INC.
219 Park Avenue South, New York, N.Y. 10003

Second Printing, 1978

Published by Arco Publishing Company, Inc.
219 Park Avenue South, New York, N.Y. 10003

Copyright © 1976 by Jack Tannen

Library of Congress Cataloging in Publication Data

Tannen, Jack
  How to identify and collect American first editions.

  1. Book Collecting. 2. Bibliography—First editions. 3. United States—Imprints.
I. Title.

Z987.T27   020'.75   76-15236

ISBN 0-668-03933-7 (Library Edition)

Printed in the United States of America

Dedicated to my wife Vivian

Preface

The history of book collecting began centuries before the invention of printing with movable metal type in the middle of the fifteenth century in Europe. In 300 B.C., Ptolemy the First built the Alexandrian library, the greatest library of ancient times. Gibbon wrote that the Emperor Gordian had twenty-two acknowledged concubines and sixty thousand volumes. While collecting books may not be as exciting as Gordian's other hobby, there *are* advantages. A fine or beautiful book retains its beauty forever, requires no maintenance beyond storage and occasional dusting, and, with the passing of years, may well become more desirable.

This book is a guide to building a collection. A collection is more than an indiscriminate assortment of odds and ends, of good and bad, of this author and that, of subjects too numerous to mention. It involves something more than mere book buying. It must have some fundamental motive. It cannot be done haphazardly, but must be done with a purpose; and collecting first editions is the name of the game.

Vincent Starrett, one of my favorite authors, whose death was a great loss to all who love books, wrote in *Books Alive* that

> Mark Twain has somewhere said that he likes a thin volume because it would steady a table, a leather volume because it would strop a razor, and a heavy book because it could be thrown at a cat. There are, of course, other purposes for which books may quite legally be employed. For example, there is as yet no law forbidding books to be read, and to be read, I think they should be purchased. And when purchased, I think they should be kept—always supposing them to be worth keeping. Thus by easy stages do I reach my subject, which is the popular diversion known as book collecting. For, while he is about it, the purchaser may just as well buy first editions and join the ranks of the elect.

Paul Jordan-Smith, in a charming book called *For the Love of Books, the Adventures of an Impecunious Collector,* had this to say about book collecting:

> To collect books for love, for information, for some past or present sentiment, for the satisfaction of intellectual curiosity, is a rational and amusing occupation. To gratify that passion by assembling the first editions of these darlings is something admirable. To join collectors' ranks for any other motive is a waste of time, money, life: the silliest of pretences, and, to say it roundly, damned rot.

I agree with the reasons Jordan-Smith offers

for collecting first editions. Book collecting is a delightful diversion, and should never be used solely for making money; but money can be made from collecting first editions when knowledge and taste are employed. Some knowledge can be acquired from this book you have in hand. Taste, however, is a faculty that can come only from experience and from the desire to master every aspect of book collecting.

Acknowledgments

Thanks are due to the many book dealers and collectors who have freely given of their time and knowledge, especially to Justin Schiller, whose knowledge of children's books far exceeds my own.

The preparation of this manuscript has been greatly helped by Mr. Harold Wehlau, whose patience and kindness have been endless.

Dr. Theodore Grieder has helped me in so many ways that I can hardly thank him enough.

Contents

Introduction

I

I think I should first point out that Jack Tannen's guide falls into two major parts:

1. The first is chiefly his "List of American Publishers and Their Methods of Denoting First Editions," which is Chapter II of this guide and is of importance not only to beginning collectors but to experienced collectors, bookmen, booksellers, and librarians as well. This "List" and its identifications of American first editions supersedes the Underhill revision of Boutell's *First Editions of Today* and will be, thus, a basic working tool for anyone working with current, out-of-print, or antiquarian books published in the U.S.

The definitions of terms in Chapter I are certainly helpful to the beginner, but I would call the attention of librarians, perhaps even forgetful collectors if such there be, to these definitions as well—particularly those for "first edition," "issue," and "state," and the illustrative examples of these terms. The quick-reference value of such definitions is obvious.

2. Chapters III through X, which make up the rest of this guide, contain bibliographical and reference material throughout. The aim of these chapters is to suggest a considerable number of fields for beginning or modest collectors and provide a sufficient framework of possibilities in book collecting and readings relevant to book collecting to lead to further exploration of these possibilities. In other words, Chapters III through X attempt to give a beginner some feel for what choices are available, what areas of collecting might be of interest to him, and, even, what particular interests of his own might serve as guidelines for collecting in new fields.

II

As Jack Tannen recognizes, any of the major areas of collecting described or suggested in his guide have called forth great numbers of historical and scholarly volumes, not to mention descriptive and enumerative bibliographies. He aims, rather, at a portable guide to American first editions and a sketch of schemes for collecting. Go to his suggested reading lists for your pleasure and intellectual profit. If you were able to acquire all of the titles he cites under their appropriate subject headings, you would then have your own useful library.

Jack Tannen also recognizes and emphasizes that a desire to make money is very far down on the list of reasons for collecting books. Man certainly does not live by bread alone, but you should collect books from personal interests; from a love for the beauty and history of print and binding; from a desire to understand the history and development (the romance, if you will) of the books in your chosen field; and from the excitement of the chase familiar to such different hunters as Nimrod, Isaac Walton, Casanova, and all book collectors of the past and present.

As a collector you will spend money. You do not know that you will ever make money, *The Wall Street Journal* and other such foolish voices to the contrary. But you do know that things *utile et dulce*—the useful and the sweet that have marked worthwhile and pleasurable vocations and avocations from classical times to the present—will be yours.

III

As a librarian I have spent a number of years building collections in both the sciences and the humanities. So I have collected more for research institutions than for myself. But if I were to recommend a beginning step in collecting, it would be to read a book that seems to me to best spell out the nature of American book collecting: Edwin Wolf and John Fleming's *Rosenbach* (Cleveland: World Publishing Co. [1960]). This remarkable biography portrays just about every aspect of the American book collecting game that anyone could think of: buying and selling, the psychology of buyer and seller, trends in literary markets and literary and collecting tastes, and the *feel* of the game. Dr. Rosenbach dealt with great varieties of books and collectors over a long period of time; and if you will look into his biography, you will discover many lessons there to be learned. Although Dr. Rosenbach was a very important bookseller, there is some of him in every bookseller in the trade today, just as there are some of the characteristics (though probably not the monetary means) of a Huntington or J.P. Morgan in every one of us who collects books.

Next, I would pick my particular area of interest and read up on it *before* I even begin to think about spending money on it. The guide you're reading contains both direct suggestions for collecting and the titles of many specialized studies that will lead you to still other books about a great many specialties and points about collecting. Then, I would decide how much I could afford to spend *without any hope of financial return*—viewing this money simply as an outlay for pure recreation.

After this, I would look into a lot of bookshops, talk to a lot of booksellers, other collectors, other book hunters, and book lovers. Asking questions, listening, and looking are very important things for the prospective and practicing collector. In addition to reading reference books, bibliographies, and other guides, I think that every collector should read the *AB (AB Bookman's Weekly)* carefully and regularly. If literature and the more serious aspects of collecting are your sort of thing, you should as well look into *The Book Collector* as a second periodical to keep up with. Certainly, attending auctions to get the feel of things is important, as is a solid understanding of such pricing guides as *American Book–Prices Current* *(ABPC)*. But here I merely repeat Jack Tannen.

I think, however, I should point out that librarians, the traditional keepers and often the purchasers of books, can sometimes be very helpful in advising from personal experience, suggesting other librarians to consult, or finding books helpful in your own field of collecting. If you can seek them out, there are librarians whose specialty is to select books and develop collections for the institution for which they work and are highly knowledgeable both about the book trade and collecting.

Finally, I would begin buying and collecting books in my chosen field of interest and knowledge. I'd proceed like a couple of amorous porcupines—very slowly and cautiously. As all experienced book collectors know, the desire to buy books grows upon them fast enough.

At whatever pace I went, I'd keep this guide around for handy reference.

T.G.

I
Aim and Scope of This Book, and Definitions of Some Basic Terms

I have been a dealer in old and rare books for almost fifty years and hope to continue for another twenty-five. Booksellers seem to live to a ripe old age, possibly due to the literary dust we are constantly breathing.

During these past years the question I have been asked most often is "How do I recognize a first edition?" To suggest an answer to this question is one of the reasons for this book. Procedures by which I attempted to arrive at such an answer are as follows:

1—Using my knowledge of the methods by which some publishers denote their first editions.
2—Checking my firm's stock to verify that knowledge.
3—Questioning my colleagues and collector clients about their understanding of the

methods used by the publishers with whom they are familiar in listing first editions.

4—Checking and rechecking my findings against copies of American first editions in the Fales Library of New York University. Because this library contains not only first editions, but second editions and variants, I was able to correct many of my findings. I owe a vote of thanks to Dr. Theodore Grieder, the curator of the collection, for permitting me to work in the stacks of the library.

5—Using the bibliographical resources of the New York Public Library to check my findings further.

6—Finally, being uncertain of the techniques used by some publishers to characterize their first editions, by writing to them to ask for clarification. Happily, all responded.

I hope that I have covered the field thoroughly; but if mistakes or omissions have occurred, your corrections or additions sent to my publisher will be gratefully received and noted for possible future revised editions.

As you will note, I have selected only those publishers who have published authors who have been and are being collected today, or who may be collected in the future.

Since this book not only covers how to identify and collect American first editions but is also a guide book, my aim will be to guide the embryo collector in choosing his subject and his authors, pointing chiefly to those within reach of his income.

To the more advanced collector who has already chosen his field, this book should contribute to the identification of first editions by more than 270 American publishers who have been publishing collected authors and Americana for over one hundred years. Also for the more advanced collector, this book lists at the end of each chapter some of the important bibliographies relating to the subject.

For the embryo collector I list below a few suggestions for his consideration in developing a focus for collecting:

1—Books, magazine articles, and miscellaneous writings of any American author.

2—Books on any phase of American history: the American Revolution; the Civil War; exploration and opening of the West; Indians, their battles and their treatment by the government; regional writing; etc.

3—American juveniles. (Sometimes difficult to determine a first edition, but a delightful and fascinating field.)

4—Private press books and fine printing.

5—Detective, Mystery, Fantasy, and Science Fiction.

6—The history and development of American industry, perhaps your own, regardless of its nature.

7—Books illustrated by American artists.

8—Books on leisure-time activity: tennis, golf, hunting, and fishing, badminton, bridge, poker, etc.

Since this is a guide book, the above are only suggestions. But whatever your choice, buy books only in good to fine condition, remembering at all times that you are building a collection of books which should bring you pleasure and, possibly, profit.

A.E. Newton, in his *Amenities of Book-Collecting and Kindred Affections,* has best expressed my feelings on collecting:

> Book-collecting is the best and safest habit there is. Best, in that it is a year-round sport and can be played at home and abroad; safest, in that when the game is called either by Father Time or the Sherriff one can get, if not all, at least a substantial part of one's money back.

Years ago, it was a simple thing to determine whether a book was a first edition. If the date on the title page corresponded with the date on the copyright page (the back of the title page, also called the verso), the book was a first edition; or, more simply, some publishers printed "First edition," "First Printing," or "First Impression" on the copyright page.

Not so today, as you will note by studying the methods used by publishers to denote their first editions. Recently, many publishers have used a device that simplifies the determination of a first edition. At the foot of the copyright page, they list consecutive numbers such as 1 2 3 4 5 6 7 8 9. If the numeral one is present, the copy is a first edition; and the lowest remaining number denotes the later edition. This system will probably be used by more and more publishers because of its simplicity and low cost.

There may be times when the date on the title page is listed as being a year later than the date on the verso. This is often due to copyright being secured in the latter part of the year. When this occurs, and no further printings are listed on the verso, the book is usually a first edition.

The definition of terms to be found in this book are mainly culled from John Carter's *A B C for Book Collectors,* an excellent and authoritative book:

Author's presentation copy is an unsigned copy of a book given by the author, possibly at the receiver's request, to someone of little or no importance.

Author's signed presentation copy is as the above but with his signature.

Author's inscribed copy is a copy signed by the author, usually in response to an owner's request.

Author's association copy, signed or unsigned, is a copy given by the author to an intimate friend, a wife, a sweetheart, or another important writer.

Bibliography—Some kind of printed history or description of books and manuscripts, with notices of the editions, the dates of printing, etc. The study of books in all phases of manufacture (ink, type, paper, binding, etc.). And, according to Webster's, "a list of writings relating to a given subject or author."

Cancels—Any part of a book substituted for the original printing, usually one or more leaves to replace defective leaves.

Colophon—A device used by the early printers and publishers to distinguish their work, usually found at the end of the book. Today it is used by some publishers to denote their first editions, and it is found on the copyright page. Many publishers who publish both limited signed and limited unsigned editions still use a colophon at the end of their books.

Copyright page, and verso—Identical terms to describe the back of the title page.

First edition—First Impression, First Printing, First edition. These terms mean the first appearance of the work in question, independently, between its own covers. Some publishers have used different systems to denote their first editions. For instance D. Appleton & Co., now Appleton-Century-Crofts, for many years used the numeral (1) at the end of the book to denote a first edition. Harcourt, Brace & Co. used the numeral (1) on the copyright page to denote a first edition. Charles Scribner's Sons used the letter (A) on the copyright page to denote a first edition.

Some first editions fall into two distinct categories: states or issues. When alterations or additions are made while the book is in press, the uncorrected book is a first state of the first edition, and the corrected book is a second or later state of the first edition. When a book is removed from the press and corrections or additions are made, or, pages are removed and cancels are substituted, then the uncorrected book is a first issue of the first edition, and the corrected book is a second or later issue of the first edition. First states and first issues are worth many times the price of later states and issues.

Format—In bibliographical terms "format" is used to indicate the size of a volume in terms of the number of times the original printed sheet has been folded. A folio has been folded once, a quarto twice, and octavo three times. This method of folding is rarely used today, but the terms still exist in catalogs. The principal formats with their common abbreviations and sizes in inches are the following:

Folio (Fo). Eighteen inches or more.
Quarto (Qto, 4to, 4°). Twelve inches or more.
Octavo (Oct., 8vo, 8°). Approximately nine inches.
Duodecimo (12mo, sometimes pronounced twelvemo). Approximately six inches.
Sextodecimo (16mo, usually pronounced sixteenmo). Approximately four inches.

Vicesimo-quarto (24mo, pronounced twentyfourmo). Approximately two inches.

Tricesimo-secundo (32mo, pronounced thirtytwomo). Approximately one inch.

Imprints—Can be determined by the publisher's name, place, and date (the three components of an "imprint") at the foot of the title page with or without the printer's name on the verso, or without the date on the title page (listed as n.d.) but with the publisher's name and occasionally the printer's name and date on the verso.

Issue—See "first edition" above; also see examples following "variants" below.

Points—Additions, deletions, or errors in printing denote points. Points are used to describe first states and first issues in first editions.

State—See "first edition" above; also see examples below.

Variants—A term used to describe different copies that exist with no known priority. Binding variants are fairly common; see below.

The following are a few examples of collected authors whose first editions are either *first states, first issues,* or *variants*:

Bellamy, Edward. *Looking Backward 2000–1887.* Boston, 1888. The first state has the printer's imprint on the copyright page. (Change made while the book was in press.)

Bierce, Ambrose. *The Dance of Death*. (San Francisco, 1877.) William Herman, pseudonym. First state has no press notices at the back of the book. (Change made while the book was in press.)

Emerson, Ralph Waldo. *Nature: An Essay and Lectures of the Times*. London, 1844. First issue has period after the first line of the title, no pages numbered 41 and 42, no imprint at foot of page 138. (Corrections made after the book was removed from the press.)

Millay, Edna St. Vincent. *Renascence*. N.Y., 1917. The first issue has paper watermarked "Glaslan." Second issue has paper watermarked "Ingres d'Arches." (Obviously, the supply of Glaslan paper ran out and the later paper was substituted.)

Steinbeck, John. *The Pastures of Heaven*. N.Y., 1932. First issue has the imprint of Brewer, Warren & Putnam. Second issue has a cancel title page with the imprint of Robert Ballou. Third issue has another cancelled title page, with the imprint of Covici Friede. This book, as you can see, has three issues; the book had been removed from the press after the first imprint and replaced for subsequent imprints.

Wallace, Lew. *Ben Hur*. N.Y., 1880. The first edition has the dedication "To the Wife of My Youth." In later editions this was changed to read "To the wife of My Youth who still abides with me." Issued with two variant bindings, a flowered cloth and plain grey cloth with bevelled edges. No known priority.

Wister, Owen. *The Virginian*. N.Y., 1902. First edition, with identical dates on the title page and verso. Variant decorations on the spine and the front cover without known priority.

Note: Whenever a date, or a place and date, are in parenthesis when listed in a dealer's or auction catalog, the information so listed is on the copyright page, not on the title page. For example, Bierce's *The Dance of Death* (San Francisco, 1877.). When the place, and/or date is listed on the title page, it will always appear without parenthesis. N.D. or n.d. denotes that the title page exists without a date, and occasionally the copyright page does too.

A jacket, listed in catalogs as d.j. or d.w., is not an integral part of a book, yet it will increase the price of a first edition many times over. An author's signature on a first edition will also increase the value of the book. An author's signed presentation copy is worth much more than a mere signed copy, and an association copy is the most valuable of all copies. An author's annotated copy has more value than a signed presentation copy, but less than an association copy. There are exceptions, of course, depending on the importance of the receiver of the book, and the number of annotations.

A word of caution—many modern authors collected today have been accepted for publication by the Book-of-the-Month Club. Some of these books could be assumed to be first editions, since they have the proper identification. However, if a small blind circle, a square, or a star is indented on the lower righthand side of the back cover, the book is not a first edition but a reprint published by the Book-of-the-Month Club. In some cases the book is not a reprint but put together from sheets obtained from the original publisher and bound by the Club. Of course, if the book has a jacket, no problem exists, since the name of the Club is printed on the jacket. Unfortunately the blind stamp does not exist on all the books of the Club, but it is present on the great majority of these books.

II
List of American Publishers and Their Methods of Denoting First Editions

A

Librarians, dealers, and collectors are often puzzled by the methods used by publishers to identify their first editions. Many of the people working for present-day publishers do not know the methods used by their firm to denote the first editions of the past. Many informed personnel have moved to other publishers; some have retired or died. A few who are themselves book collectors can sometimes arrive at the correct answer.

H.S. Boutel, in 1928, wrote *First Editions of Today and How to Tell Them*. It has had four editions, the last in 1965, and is now out-of-print. The book you now have in hand is not a revision of Boutel but a completely new book. It covers American publishers of today and those that were publishing over a hundred years ago. It also has eight additional chapters on collecting first editions of various kinds and includes bibliographies. The methods used to determine the identifications below have been explained in the first chapter.

These are the publishers and their identification of first editions:

Alliance Book Corporation. The first edition does not list additional printings on the copyright page.

Henry Altemus. The first edition is identified by identical dates on the title page and verso.

American Publishing Company. The first edition is identified by identical dates on the title page and verso or the date on the title page is listed as one year later than the date on the verso, without additional printings listed on that page.

D. Appleton & Co. Now Appleton-Century-Crofts. The first edition is denoted by a "1" at the foot of the last page of text or by "First Edition" on the copyright page.

Arcadia House. The first edition does not list additional printings on the copyright page.

Arco Publishing Co. Inc. The first edition does not list additional printings on the copyright page.

Arkham House. The first edition is identified by identical dates on the title page and verso.

Argus Books, Inc. or Ben Abramson, Publisher. The first edition does not list additional printings on the copyright page.

Atheneum Publishers. "First Edition" is printed on the copyright page.

The Atlantic Monthly Press. Until 1925, when all publications were issued under its own imprint, the first edition was identified by the lack of additional printings on the copyright page. Since 1925, under the Little, Brown imprint, the first edition can be identified in two ways: identical dates on the title page and verso; or without the date on the title page, but with "First Edition" on the verso.

Richard G. Badger. The first edition can be identified by identical dates on the title page and verso.

The Baker & Taylor Company. The first edition can be identified by identical dates on the title page and verso.

Robert D. Ballou, Publisher; Robert Ballou, Inc. "First Published (with date)" on the copyright page.

A.S. Barnes & Co. Inc. The first edition is identified by identical dates on the title page and verso.

Richard W. Baron Publishing Co. Inc. "First Published" on the copyright page.

Barre Publishing Company, Inc. The first edition can be identified by identical dates on the title page and verso.

M. Barrows & Company. "First Printing" is listed on the copyright page.

Beacon Press. The first edition does not list additional printings on the copyright page.

Beechurst Press, Inc.; Bernard Ackerman, Inc. The first edition does not list additional printings on the copyright page.

The Bobbs-Merrill Company, Inc. It is extremely difficult to determine the identification of their first editions. Some books have later printings listed on the copyright page; some have "First Edition" or month only on the copyright page. I suggest you check the appropriate bibliographies to be sure.

Albert & Charles Boni or Boni & Gaer, Inc. The first edition can be identified by identical dates on the title page and verso or without additional printings listed on that page.

Boni & Liveright. "First Edition" on the copyright page or identical dates on the title page and verso.

The Bowen–Merrill Company. The first edition can be identified by the date on the title page, which may, in some cases, be one year later than the date on the copyright page, but without additional printings on the title page or verso.

R.R. Bowker Company. The first edition does not list additional printings on the copyright page.

George Braziller, Inc. "First Printing" is listed on the copyright page.

Brentano's. Before 1927, later printings were listed on the copyright page. In 1928 and later "First Edition" was listed on that page.

Brewer & Warren or Brewer, Warren & Putnam. The first edition can be identified by identical dates on the title page and verso or without additional printings on the copyright page.

Broadside Press. "First Edition" is listed on the copyright page.

Cameron Associates. The first edition does not list additional printings on the copyright page.

The Candlelight Press. The first edition can be identified by identical dates on the title page and verso.

Jonathan Cape & Harrison Smith. "First Published (with year)" is listed on the copyright page corresponding with the copyright date.

The Cardavon Press, Inc. Publishers of Limited Editions. Editions denoted in a colophon in the back of the book.

G.W. Carleton. The first edition can be identified by identical dates on the title page and verso or the date on the title page can be one year later than the date on the copyright page without additional printings listed on that page.

Carrick and Evans, Inc. The letter "A" on the copyright page denotes the first edition.

Caxton Printers, Ltd. The first edition can be identified by identical dates on the title page and verso. In joint publishing, the first edition can be identified by the name of Caxton Printers above the other publisher at the foot of the title page.

The Century Co. The first edition can be identified by identical dates on the title page and verso, or, "First Printing" on the verso, or n.d. on the title page without additional printings on the copyright page, or "Published (month & year)" on the copyright page corresponding with the copyright date.

Citadel Press. "First Edition" on the copyright page or without additional printings listed on the page.

C.M. Clark Publishing Co. The first edition can be identified by identical dates on the title page and verso.

Edward J. Clode, Inc. The first edition can be identified by identical dates on the title page and verso or n.d. on the title page without additional printings listed on the copyright page.

Henry T. Coates & Co. The first edition can be identified by "Published (month and year)" on the copyright page corresponding with the copyright date.

Columbia University Press. The first edition lists a date on the title page; in second and later printings the date is removed.

Lewis Copeland Company. The first edition can be identified by "First Printing (month and year)" on the copyright page corresponding with the copyright date.

Copeland and Day. The first edition can be identified by identical dates on the title page and verso.

Cornell University Press. The first edition can be identified by "First Published (with year)" on the copyright page corresponding with the copyright date.

Cosmopolitan Book Corporation. The first edition can be identified by identical dates on the title page and verso.

The Countryman Press. Publishers of limited and non-limited first editions. Limited edition notice is usually on the page facing the title page. The first edition does not list additional printings on the copyright page.

Covici Friede and Pascal Covici. The first edition can be identified by identical dates on the title page and verso or "First Edition" on the copyright page.

Covici–McGee, Publishers. "First Printing" is listed on the copyright page.

Coward–McCann, Inc.; Coward, McCann & Geoghegan, Inc. The first edition can be identified by identical dates on the title page and verso or "First Edition" on the copyright page.

Creative Age Press, Inc. The first edition can be identified by identical dates on the title page and verso or n.d. without additional printings listed on that page.

Thomas Y. Crowell Company, Inc. "First Printing" is listed on the copyright page, or, without later printings on the title page or verso or in other editions, the numbers at the foot of the copyright page should include the number "1" to be a first edition.

Crown Publishers, Inc. The first edition does not list additional printings on the copyright page.

Dartmouth Publications. The first edition can be identified by identical dates on the title page and verso.

Dawson's Book Shop. Most of their publications have appeared in one edition only, later editions are clearly indicated as such.

The John Day Company, Inc. "First Published (month & year)" on the copyright page corresponding with the copyright date or n.d. without additional printings on that page.

Stephen Daye Press. The first edition does not list additional printings on the copyright page.

Delacorte Press. "First Printing" on the copyright

page or n.d. without additional printings listed on that page.

The Derrydale Press, Inc. Printers of limited editions only, with the number of copies printed listed on the copyright page or on the colophon at the end of the book.

The Dial Press. The first edition can be identified by identical dates on the title page and verso or "First Printing" on that page.

Didier, Publishers. The first edition does not list additional printings on the copyright page.

The Dietz Press. "First Edition" on the copyright page or n.d. without additional printings listed on that page.

G.W. Dillingham Company. The first edition can be identified by identical dates on the title page and verso or "Issued (month & year)" on the copyright page corresponding with the copyright date.

Dodd Mead & Company. The first edition can be identified by identical dates on the title page and verso or n.d. without additional printings listed on that page.

B.W. Dodge & Company. The first edition can be identified by identical dates on the title page and verso.

Dodge Publishing Company. "First Edition" is printed on the copyright page.

George H. Doran & Co. "First Printing," or, GHD colophon on the copyright page denote the first edition.

Dorrance & Co. Inc. "First Edition" on the copyright page or n.d. without later printings on that page.

Doubleday & Company, Inc. or Doubleday, Doran & Company. "First Edition" is printed on the copyright page.

Doubleday, Page & Company. "First Edition" on the copyright page or identical dates on the title page and verso.

Duell, Sloane & Pearce. "First Edition" or "First Printing" on the copyright page or the Roman numeral "I" on that page denote the first edition.

Duffield & Co., later Duffield & Green. The first edition can be identified by identical dates on the title page and verso, or "First Edition" sometimes printed on that page, or n.d. without additional printings listed on that page.

Duke University Press. The first edition does not list additional printings on the copyright page.

Dunster House Bookshop. The first edition can be identified by identical dates on the title page and verso.

Philip C. Duschnes. The first edition can be identified by identical dates on the title page and verso.

E.P. Dutton & Co. Inc. The first edition can be identified by identical dates on the title page and verso, or identical dates but with "First Edition" on the copyright page, or n.d. but with "First Edition" on that page.

Eaton & Mains. The first edition can be identified by identical dates on the title page and verso.

Equinox Cooperative Press, Inc. The first edition does not list additional printings on the copyright page. The limited editions are listed on the same page.

Falmouth Publishing House, Inc. The first edition does not list additional printings on the copyright page.

Farrar & Rinehart, Inc.; Farrar Straus & Company; Farrar Straus & Cudahy; Farrar, Straus & Giroux, Inc. The first edition could be identified in their early editions by the colophon on the copyright page, later and at the present time "First Printing" or "First Edition" is listed on that page.

Frederick Fell Publishers, Inc. "First Printing (month & year)" is listed on the copyright page.

Fields, Osgood & Co. The first edition can be identified by identical dates on the title page and verso.

The Fine Editions Press. The first edition can be identified by identical dates on the title page and verso.

Follett Publishing Company. "First Printing" is listed on the copyright page.

Four Seas Company. The first edition does not list additional printings on the copyright page.

Funk & Wagnalls Inc. "First Published (month & year)" on the copyright page, or the numeral "1" after the copyright date, or without the numeral but no listing of additional printings on that page denote the first edition.

Lee Furman, Inc. No attempt is made to distinguish first from later editions.

Gambit. "First Printing" is listed on the copyright page.

Bernard Geis Associates. "First Printing" is listed on the copyright page.

The Gnome Press, Inc. "First Edition" is printed on the copyright page.

William Godwin. The first edition does not list additional printings on the copyright page.

Laurence J. Gomme. The first edition can be identified by identical dates on the title page and verso.

The Grafton Press. N.d. on the title page, month and year on the copyright page identical with the copyright date identifies the first edition.

Greenberg, Publisher, Inc. The first edition does not list additional printings on the copyright page.

Grove Press, Inc. "First Printing" is listed on the copyright page.

Hale, Cushman & Flint, Inc. All editions are noted on the copyright page.

The Hampshire Bookshop, Inc. The first edition does not list additional printings on the copyright page.

Harcourt, Brace & Co. Inc.; Harcourt, Brace &

World; Harcourt, Brace, Jovanovich, Inc. Three methods have been used to determine the first edition:

1—N.d. on the title page and the numeral "1" on the copyright page.

2—N.d. and "Published (month & year)" on the copyright page identical with copyright date.

3—In recent years "First Edition" is listed on the copyright page. On rare occasions, identical dates on the title page and verso.

Frances P. Harper. The first edition is identified by a date on the title page without additional listings on the verso.

Harper & Row, Publisher; Harper & Brothers; Harper & Row, Peterson. The following information was sent to me by Harper & Row: The words "First Edition" are printed on the copyright page and are removed from later printings. This practice was started in May, 1922. In the period 1922 to 1960, some books, if they were not printed in letterpress, did not use this expression and priority is difficult to determine. It has been the practice in recent years to indicate FIRST U.S. EDITION if the book was published earlier in Great Britain. In addition to the first-edition marking, Harper & Brothers used a letter code to indicate the month and year of printing.

The code was occasionally omitted prior to

the merger with Row, Peterson in 1964 and
seems to have been mostly omitted shortly
after. The code was started in 1912 and refers
to printing only and has no reference to copyright. The month was listed first:

A-January	G-July
B-February	H-August
C-March	I-September
D-April	K-October
E-May	L-November
F-June	M-December

M-1912	Y-1924	L-1936	X-1948	K-1960
N-1913	Z-1925	M-1937	Y-1949	L-1961
O-1914	A-1926	N-1938	Z-1950	M-1962
P-1915	B-1927	O-1939	A-1951	N-1963
Q-1916	C-1928	P-1940	B-1952	O-1964
R-1917	D-1929	Q-1941	C-1953	P-1965
S-1918	E-1930	R-1942	D-1954	Q-1966
T-1919	F-1931	S-1943	E-1955	R-1967
U-1920	G-1932	T-1944	F-1956	S-1968
V-1921	H-1933	U-1945	G-1957	T-1969
W-1922	I-1934	V-1946	H-1958	U-1970
X-1923	K-1935	W-1947	I-1959	V-1971

On rare occasions, the words "First Printing"
were used on the copyright page. The first
edition marking was usually omitted from
children's picture books. Before 1922, the
first edition could be identified by identical

dates on the title page and verso, or, "Published (month & year)" on the copyright page corresponding with the copyright date. Since 1973 Harper has generally used the printing number/year code that is becoming common in the industry. Such as 7576777810 987654321. The numbers on the left are years and the numbers on the right denote the edition. Since the number one is present in the above code, the book is a first edition; in a second printing the numeral one is dropped and the lowest number on the right would be the number two.

Harvard University Press. The first edition can be identified by identical dates on the title page and verso, or n.d. without additional printings listed on that page.

Hastings House Publishers, Inc. The first edition does not list additional printings on the copyright page.

Rae D. Henkle Co. Inc.; The Henkle–Yewdale House, Inc. The first edition does not list additional printings on the copyright page.

Hermes Publications. "First Edition" listed on the copyright page or without later printings on that page.

Hermitage House. "First Edition" is listed on the copyright page.

Hill & Wang. All editions are listed on the copyright page.

Hillman–Curl, Inc. The first edition does not list additional printings on the copyright page.

Holiday House, Inc. The first edition does not list additional printings on the copyright page.

Henry Holt & Company, Inc.; Holt, Rinehart & Winston, Inc. "First Printing" or "First Edition" is listed on the copyright page, or "Published (month & year)" on the same page corresponding with the copyright date, or n.d. without additional printings listed on the copyright page.

Horizon Press. The first edition does not list additional printings on the copyright page.

Houghton Mifflin Company. The first edition can be identified by identical dates on the title page and verso or "First Printing (month & year)" on the copyright page corresponding with the copyright date.

Howell Soskin, Publishers. The first edition does not list additional printings on the copyright page.

B.W. Huebsch. The first edition can be identified by identical dates on the title page and verso.

Bruce Humphries, Inc. The first edition does not list additional printings on the copyright page.

The Huntington Library; Henry E. Huntington Library and Art Gallery. The first edition can be identified by identical dates on the title page and verso or without later printings on the copyright page.

The Imprint Society. Each edition of the Society is limited to 1950 copies and is not reprinted.

Indiana University Press. Until 1974 the first edition did not list additional printings on the copyright page. From 1974 until the unforseeable future, the numbers from one to ten will be on the copyright page. Number one will denote a first edition; if it is removed the lowest remaining number will denote the edition.

Iowa State University Press. The first edition does not list additional printings on the copyright page.

The Johns Hopkins University Press. The first edition does not list additional printings on the copyright page.

Marshall Jones Company. The first edition does not list additional printings on the copyright page; occasionally "First Edition" is listed on that page.

Claude Kendall, Inc.; Claude Kendall & Willoughby Sharp, Inc. "First Edition" or "First Printing" is listed on the copyright page.

Mitchell Kennerly. The first edition can be identified by identical dates on the title page and verso.

Kent State University Press. "First Edition" is printed on the copyright page.

King's Crown Press. The first edition can be identified by the date on the title page which is removed in later editions.

H.C. Kinsey & Company, Inc. The first edition does not list additional printings on the copyright page.

Alfred A. Knopf, Inc. The first edition can be identified by identical dates on the title page and verso or without later printings listed on the copyright page. Later, and at the present time, "First Edition" is printed on the copyright page.

John Lane Company. The first edition can be identified by identical dates on the title page and verso.

Lantern Press, Inc. The first edition does not list additional printings on the copyright page.

Lee and Shepard. The first edition can be identified by identical dates on the title page and verso or "Published (month & year)" on the copyright page corresponding with the copyright date.

J.B. Lippincott Company. "First Edition" or "Published (month & year)" on the copyright page corresponding with the copyright date.

Little, Brown and Company. "First Edition" on the copyright page or identical dates on the title page and verso.

Horace Liveright, Inc.; Liveright Publishing Corp. The first edition does not list additional printings on the copyright page, occasionally "First Edition" is listed on that page.

Longmans, Green & Co. "First Edition" is listed on the copyright page or identical dates on the title page and verso.

Loring & Mussey, Inc. "First Edition" is printed on the copyright page or without further printings on that page.

Lothrop Publishing Company. The first edition can be identified by identical dates on the title page and verso or without further printings listed on that page.

Lothrop, Lee & Shepard Company, Inc. The first edition can be identified by "Published (month & year)" on the copyright page identical with the copyright date or without additional printings listed on that page.

Louisiana State University Press. The first edition does not list additional printings on the copyright page.

John W. Luce & Company. The first edition can be identified by identical dates on the title page and verso or without additional printings listed on that page.

The Macauley Company. The first edition does not list additional printings on the copyright page.

Robert M. McBride & Company. "First Edition" is listed on the copyright page, or "First Published (month & year)" or "Published (month & year)" on that page corresponding with the copyright date.

The McClure Company; McClure, Phillips & Co. The first edition can be identified by identical dates on the title page and verso, or "Published (month & year)," or "First Impression (month & year)" on the copyright page corresponding with the copyright date.

A.C. McClurg & Co. The first edition can be identified by "Published (month & year)" on the copyright page corresponding with the copyright date.

mcdowell obolensky. "First Printing" is listed on the copyright page or n.d. without further printings listed on that page.

McGraw Hill Book Company. "First Edition" is listed on the copyright page, or n.d. without further printings listed on that page, or numbers one to nine printed at the foot of the copyright page with the lowest number denoting the edition.

David McKay Co. Inc. The first edition does not list additional printings on the copyright page.

Macmillan, Inc. and Macmillan Company. "First Printing" is listed on the copyright page, or identical dates on the title page and verso, or "Published (month & year)" on the copyright page identical with the copyright date. There is at least one variation, possibly more, with the latter identification. The one best known is in the first edition of Margaret Mitchell's *Gone With the Wind*. In most copies the copyright page reads "Published, June, 1936" whereas the first edition, first issue should read "Published, May, 1936."

McNally & Loftin, Publishers. The first edition does not list additional printings on the copyright page.

Macrae Smith Company. "First Printing" is listed on the copyright page or without additional printings listed on that page.

Macy–Masius. The first edition can be identified by identical dates on the title page and verso or "Published (with year)" on the copyright page corresponding with the copyright date.

Frank Maurice. The first edition can be identified by identical dates on the title page and verso.

Merlin Press, Inc. The first edition can be identified by identical dates on the title page and verso.

Julian Messner. The first edition does not list additional printings on the copyright page.

Minnesota Historical Society. Before 1940, no consistent plan was used to identify first editions. After 1940, the first edition does not list additional printings on the copyright page.

Minton, Balch & Co. The first edition can be identified by identical dates on the title page and verso.

Modern Age Books. The first edition can be identified by identical dates on the title page and verso.

Moffat, Yard and Company. The first edition can be identified by "Published (month & year)" on the copyright page corresponding with the copyright date.

William Morrow & Co. Inc. The first edition can be identified by identical dates on the title page and verso, or "First Printing (month & year)" on the copyright page corresponding with the copyright date, or without further printings listed on that page.

Barrows Mussey, Inc. Either "First Edition" or without further printings listed on the copyright page.

Mycroft & Moran. The first edition can be identified by identical dates on the title page and verso.

Nash Publishing Corporation. "First Printing" is listed on the copyright page.

Naylor Company. The first edition does not list additional printings on the copyright page.

Walter Neale and The Neale Publishing Company. The first edition can be identified by identical dates on the title page and verso.

F. Tennyson Neely. The first edition can be identified by identical dates on the title page and verso.

The New American Library, Inc. "First Printing (month & year)" on the copyright page identical with the copyright date.

New Directions Publishing Corporation. It is difficult to determine the methods used by this company to denote their first editions. In answer to my inquiry, this was their response: "If a book does not say second, third, etc., printing on the copyright page, it can be assumed it is a first edition."

Northwestern University Press. The first edition can be identified by identical dates on the title page and verso.

W.W. Norton & Company, Inc. "First Edition" is printed on the copyright page or a list of numbers from one to ten at the foot of that page. The lowest number denotes the edition.

Noyes, Platt & Company. The first edition can be identified by identical dates on the title page and verso.

Ivan Obolensky. "First Edition" is printed on the copyright page.

The Odyssey Press, Inc. "First Edition" is printed

on the copyright page or alphabetical letters for revision and ascending numbers for printing: A 1 would be a first edition, later numbers would denote later printings.

Ohio State University Press. The first edition does not list additional printings on the copyright page.

Ohio University Press. The first edition can be identified by identical dates on the title page and verso or "n.d." without additional printings listed on the copyright page.

James R. Osgood and Company. The first edition can be identified by identical dates on the title page and verso.

Oxford University Press, Inc. "First Edition" is printed on the copyright page, or without further printings listed on that page.

L.C. Page & Co. "First Impression (month & year)" or "First Printing" listed on the copyright page.

Pantheon Books, Inc. "First Edition" or "First Printing" listed on the copyright page or without further printings listed on that page.

Payson & Clarke, Ltd. The first edition can be identified by identical dates on the title page and verso or without additional printings listed on that page.

Pellegrini and Cudahy. The first edition does not list additional printings on the copyright page.

The Penn Publishing Company. The first edition can be identified by identical dates on the title page and verso or the date on the title page can be one year later than the copyright date without additional printings listed on the copyright page.

William Penn Publishing Company. The first edition does not list additional printings on the copyright page.

Pergamon Press, Inc. "First Edition" is printed on the copyright page.

Peter Pauper Press. Earlier, all books published by this press were limited editions and were so listed. At the present time the press has been publishing reprints, and when the edition is original, no attempt has been made to denote the first edition.

Clarkson N. Potter, Inc. "First Edition" is printed on the copyright page.

Press of the Western Reserve University. The first edition does not list additional printings on the copyright page.

Princeton University Press. The first edition does

not list additional printings on the copyright page.

G.P. Putnam's Sons. The first edition can be identified by identical dates on the title page and verso or n.d. without further printings listed on that page.

Rand McNally & Company. "First Printing (month & year)" on the copyright page identical with the copyright date or without further printings listed on that page.

Random House, Inc. "First Edition" or "First Printing" on the copyright page.

The Reilly & Britton Co. The first edition can be identified by identical dates on the title page and verso or without further printings listed on that page.

The Reilly & Lee Co. Inc. "First Printing" is listed on the copyright page or without further printings on that page.

Fleming H. Revell Company. The first edition can be identified by identical dates on the title page and verso.

Reynal and Hitchcock, Inc. "First Edition" is printed on the copyright page or without additional printings listed on that page.

Roberts Brothers. The first edition can be identified by identical dates on the title page and verso.

Roy Publishers, Inc. The first edition does not list additional printings on the copyright page.

William Edwin Rudge. The first edition can be identified by identical dates on the title page and verso.

R.H. Russell. "First Impression (month & year)" on the copyright page identical with the copyright date or identical dates on the title page and verso.

Rutgers University Press. The first edition does not list additional printings on the copyright page.

Sagamore Press. The first edition does not list additional printings on the copyright page.

Sage Books, Inc. (Imprint of Alan Swallow, Publisher). The first edition does not list additional printings on the copyright page.

St. Martin's Press, Inc. The first edition does not list additional printings on the copyright page.

Henry Schuman, Inc.; Abelard-Schuman, Ltd. The first edition does not list additional printings on the copyright page.

Charles Scribner's Sons. Before 1929, a first
edition could be identified in two ways—by
identical dates on the title page and verso, or
without later printings listed on that page.
After 1929 and before 1973, a first edition had
the letter "A" on the copyright page, removed
or replaced by "B," "C," etc., in later editions.
Today, the following or similar notations can
be found on the copyright page "1 3 5 h/c 6 4
2." The letters indicate cloth or paper and a
code for the binder. The lowest number on
either side of the letter code indicates the
printing. As you can see, in the above, the
numeral one being present, the book is a first
edition. If it were lacking, the lowest number
remaining on either side of the letter code (h/c)
would denote the edition.

Sears Publishing Company, Inc. The first edition
does not list additional printings on the copyright page.

Thomas Seltzer. The first edition can be identified by identical dates on the title page and
verso.

Sheed & Ward, Inc. The first edition can be identified by identical dates on the title page and
verso.

Sheridan House, Inc. The first edition can be
identified by identical dates on the title page

and verso or without additional printings listed on that page.

Sherman, French & Company. The first edition can be identified by identical dates on the title page and verso.

Silver Burdett Company. The first edition can be identified by identical dates on the title page and verso.

Simon & Schuster, Inc. "First Printing" is listed on the copyright page or without further printings listed on that page.

Small Maynard and Company. The first edition can be identified by identical dates on the title page and verso.

William Sloane Associates, Inc. "First Printing" is listed on the copyright page.

Harrison Smith, Inc.; Harrison Smith & Robert Haas, Inc. "First Printing" is listed on the copyright page, or identical dates on the title page and verso, or n.d. without additional printings listed on that page.

Richard R. Smith. The first edition can be identified by identical dates on the title page and verso or n.d. without additional printings listed on that page.

Something Else Press. The first edition can be identified by identical dates on the title page and verso.

Southern Illinois University Press. The first edition does not list additional printings on the copyright page.

Southwest Press. The first edition can be identified by identical dates on the title page and verso.

Stackpole Books; Stackpole Company; Stackpole Sons'. "First Edition" on the copyright page or without further printings listed on that page.

Stanford University Press. The first edition does not list additional printings on the copyright page.

Stanton and Lee. The first edition can be identified by identical dates on the title page and verso.

State Historical Society of Wisconsin. The first edition does not list additional printings on the copyright page.

Stein & Day, Publishers. The first edition does not list additional printings on the copyright page.

George W. Stewart, Publisher, Inc. The first edition does not list additional printings on the copyright page.

Frederick A. Stokes & Co. The first edition can be identified by identical dates on the title page and verso or without later printings listed on that page.

Herbert S. Stone & Co.; Stone and Kimball. The first edition can be identified by identical dates on the title page and verso.

The Sunwise Turn. The first edition can be identified by identical dates on the title page and verso.

Superior Publishing Company. The first edition does not list additional printings on the copyright page.

The Swallow Press Inc.; Alan Swallow, Publisher. "First Printing (month & year)" on the copyright page identical with the copyright date or without additional printings listed on that page.

Syracuse University Press. The first edition does not list additional printings on the copyright page.

Taplinger Publishing Co. Inc. "First Published Edition" is printed on the copyright page.

The Third Press. "First Printing" is listed on the copyright page.

Ticknor and Company; Ticknor & Fields. The first edition can be identified by identical dates on the title page and verso or the date on the title page can be one year later than the copyright date without additional printings listed on the copyright page.

Trail's End Publishing Co. All editions are noted on the copyright page.

Trident Press. The first edition can be identified by identical dates on the title page and verso or the date on the title page can be one year later than the copyright date without additional printings listed on the copyright page.

Twayne Publishers, Inc. The first edition does not list additional printings on the copyright page.

Frederick Ungar Publishing Co. Inc. The first edition does not list additional printings on the copyright page.

University of Alabama Press. The first edition does not list additional printings on the copyright page.

The University of Arizona Press. The first edition does not list additional printings on the copyright page.

University of California Press. The first edition can be identified by identical dates on the title page and verso or without later printings listed on that page.

University of Chicago Press. The first edition can be identified by n.d. on the title page and "Published (month & year)" on the copyright page without later printings listed on that page.

University of Colorado Press. The first edition does not list additional printings on the copyright page.

University of Illinois Press. For titles published between 1918 and 1950, the earliest publication date is almost certain to indicate the first and only printing. Since 1950, succeeding printings are so indicated either on the title page (occasionally) or on the copyright page.

University of Kentucky Press. The first edition does not list additional printings on the copyright page.

University of Miami Press. The first edition does not list additional printings on the copyright page.

The University of Michigan Press. Since 1960 title pages have not been dated and the first edition does not have additional printings on the copyright page.

University of Minnesota Press. The first edition does not list additional printings on the copyright page.

University of Nebraska Press. The first edition does not list additional printings on the copyright page.

The University of North Carolina Press. The first edition can be identified by identical dates on the title page and verso or without additional printings listed on that page.

University of Oklahoma Press. "First Edition" is printed on the copyright page.

University of Pennsylvania Press. The first edition can be identified by identical dates on the title page and verso or without additional printings listed on that page.

University of Pittsburgh Press. The first edition does not list additional printings on the copyright page.

University of South Carolina Press. "First Edition" is printed on the copyright page.

University of Tennessee Press. The first edition does not list additional printings on the copyright page.

University of Texas Press. The first edition does not list additional printings on the copyright page.

The University Press of Virginia. The first edition can be identified by identical dates on the title page and verso.

University of Washington Press. The first edition does not list later printings on the copyright page.

Vanderbilt University Press. The first edition does not list additional printings on the copyright page.

The Vanguard Press, Inc. The first edition does not list additional printings on the copyright page.

The Viking Press, Inc. "First Published" or "Published (month & year)" on the copyright page or identical dates on the title page and verso.

Frederick Warne & Co. Inc. First editions are identified by the appearance of the numbers one to ten at the foot of the copyright page. Similarly, later numbers denote later editions.

Ives Washburn, Inc. The first edition can be identified by identical dates on the title page and verso or without additional printings listed on that page.

G. Howard Watt. The first edition does not list additional printings on the copyright page.

Franklin Watts, Inc. "First Edition" is printed on the copyright page, or identical dates on the title page and verso, or numerals from one up listed at the foot of the copyright page. If the numeral one is present the book is a first edition; higher numerals denote later editions.

Way and Williams. The first edition can be identified by identical dates on the title page and verso.

Charles L. Webster and Company. The first edition can be identified by identical dates on the title page and verso.

Wesleyan University Press. "First Edition" is printed on the copyright page.

Weybright and Talley, Inc. The first edition does not list additional printings on the copyright page.

Whittlesey House. "First Edition" on the copyright page or without additional printings listed on that page.

W.A. Wilde Company. The first edition does not list additional printings on the copyright page.

Willett, Clark & Company. The first edition does not list additional printings on the copyright page.

The H.W. Wilson Company. The first edition can be identified by identical dates on the title page and verso, plus "Published (month & year)" on the same page or without additional printings listed on that page.

John C. Winston Co. The first edition does not list additional printings on the copyright page.

World Publishing Company. "First Edition" or "First Printing" is listed on the copyright page.

A.A. Wyn, Inc. The first edition does not list additional printings on the copyright page.

Yale University Press. "First Published (month & year)" printed on the copyright page corresponding with the copyright date or without additional printings listed on that page.

Zero Press. "First Edition" is printed on the copyright page.

Ziff-Davis Publishing Company. The first edition does not list additional printings on the copyright page.

B. Bibliographical Note

These are the identifications of first editions by American publishers. Some of the answers I received to the inquiries sent to many of these publishers left me doubting that the respondent knew the previous methods used by his publisher to denote first editions. I would suggest that you consult the bibliography of the individual author, if it exists, or the bibliographies of American literature if you are at all in doubt about whether or not the book you have or are thinking of buying is a correct first edition.

The first bibliographer of a comprehensive collection of American first editions was P.K. Foley, a bookseller of Boston, who resented the fact that American collectors were far more interested in English first editions than in those of their countrymen. To remedy this situation he wrote a bibliography of American writers covering the period from 1795 to 1895. The book was published in 1897. Its main emphasis was on the writers of New England, including Emerson, Lowell, Thoreau, Whittier, and others of equal and lesser importance.

In 1922, Merle Johnson asked authorities in the field of American bibliography to identify the first editions of those writers, new and old, whom they considered important enough to be made available in book form for the use of scholars, collectors, librarians, and booksellers. The results of this inquiry were printed in *Publisher's Weekly* (the journal of the book trade) from September 9, 1922, to May 24, 1941. The first edition of Merle Johnson's *American First Editions* was published in April, 1929. Johnson kept revising and enlarging his book from the articles in *Publisher's Weekly*, and in 1932 he brought out a second revised edition. He was still working on another revision when he died in 1935. Jacob Blanck continued the work and his first revised edition, which was the third edition of Johnson's, appeared in 1936. The fourth revised, and Blanck's last edition of Merle Johnson, was published in 1942.

With the authorization of Jacob Blanck, who has since died, Joseph Katz is preparing a completely new edition of Johnson's *American First Editions*, and his method of revision is similar to that undertaken by Merle Johnson in 1922. He has sent out a letter of invitation to collectors, booksellers, librarians, and anyone else seriously interested in American author bibliography to participate in making *The New Merle Johnson's American First Editions*, which will be the fifth edition and will be published by G.K. Hall of Boston. Mr. Katz has this to say:

My goal is to make the *New Merle Johnson's American First Editions* continue the tradition of utility upheld by its ancestors. There are, I think, three features on which that tradition is based. First, it serves our continuing need to have bibliographical information for scores of authors distilled into one volume that is a handy working tool. Second, the authors it covers are those in whom the contemporary generation of book people have active interest. And, third, those very same book people are invited to serve as the "panel of experts" who contribute information to the making of the authors' bibliographies.

With the death of Jacob Blanck, America lost its most important and most thorough bibliographer on the work of American writers. Besides the two revisions of the work of Merle Johnson, which he made in 1936 and 1942, Blanck is also noted for his *Peter Parley to Penrod, a Bibliographical Description of the Best-loved American Juvenile Books.* But foremost is his monumental *Bibliography of American Literature,* which he compiled for the Bibliographical Society of America. He began this work in 1950, and the first volume which covered the writings of Henry Adams to Donn Byrne was published by the Yale University Press in 1955. Volume Six, bringing the *BAL* from Henry Adams to Thomas William Parsons, was published in 1973. Subsequent volumes, containing much work supervised by Blanck, should bring the *BAL* to conclusion; but the hand that guided this bibliographical labor of love for twenty-three years will be sorely missed.

With the increasing interest in bibliographical studies, I believe that in a few years every important American writer, including those who have written detective stories, fantasy, and science fiction, will be included in some bibliography of

American literature. In the meantime, here are some of the best bibliographies available at present:

Bennett, Whitman. *A Practical Guide to American Book Collecting (1663-1940)* N.Y. (1941).

Blanck, Jacob. *Bibliography of American Literature.* Compiled for the Bibliographical Society of America. Volume one: Henry Adams to Donn Byrne. New Haven, 1955; to volume six: Augustus Baldwin Longstreet to Thomas William Parsons. New Haven, 1973. Six volumes published thus far.

Brussel, I.R. *Anglo–American First Editions.* Volume two, *West to East, 1786-1930.* First editions of American authors whose books were first published in England. N.Y., 1936.

Foley, P.K. *American Authors 1795-1895. A Bibliography of First and Notable Editions.* Boston, 1897.

Johnson, Merle. *American First Editions.* 4th edition, revised and enlarged by Jacob Blanck. N.Y., 1942. Forthcoming: *The New Merle Johnson's American First Editions.* 5th ed. revised by Joseph Katz. Boston, G.K. Hall.

Miller, Leon. *American First Editions, Their Points and Prices.* Kansas City, Mo., 1937. An interesting book; the prices should be compared with those of the present day to indicate the rise and fall in values of the listed authors.

Nilon, C.H. *Bibliography of Bibliographies in American Literature.* N.Y., 1970.

Shaw, R.R., & Shoemaker, R.H. *American Bibliography, a Preliminary Checklist (1801–1819)*. N.Y. 1958–1965. Volumes one to nineteen and addenda in progress.

Spiller, R.E. & Others (eds.), *Literary History of the U.S.* N.Y., 1974. (Volume three only—the bibliography.)

Stone, H.S. *First Editions of American Authors. A Manual for Book-Lovers*. With a Bibliography. Kennebunkport, Me., 1970.

Targ, William. *American First Editions and Their Prices from 1640 to the Present Day*. Chicago, 1931. An excellent book, the prices should be compared with those of the present day.

Targ, William. *Ten Thousand Rare Books and Their Prices. A Dictionary of First Editions and Their Prices*. Chicago, 1936. This book contains listings of authors other than American, and his choices are excellent. Compare the prices with those of today.

Wright, Lyle H. *American Fiction 1774–1850. A Contribution Toward a Bibliography*. Revised edition. San Marino, 1948.

Wright, Lyle H. *American Fiction 1851–1875. A Contribution Toward a Bibliography*. San Marino, 1957.

Wright, Lyle H. *American Fiction 1876–1900. A Contribution Toward a Bibliography*. San Marino, 1966.

The last three books above are far more than a contribution toward a bibliography. They do not indicate first issues or first states of first editions, but they do locate copies in particular libraries. From that, one can estimate the relative scarcity of any book listed, although Wright's locations are far from complete (the Fales Library, among others, not being recorded).

III
Collecting Americana

Interest in collecting Americana has increased tremendously in the last fifty years, and the prices at auction and in dealer's catalogs demonstrate that, despite depression and recession, books have risen far above their value since the 1920s. This is particularly true in the fields of Western Americana and exploration.

There are still many fields in Americana that have not as yet increased appreciably in value, but offer fertile territory to the collector with imagination, vision, and patience. An essential book for the beginner, or even for the more advanced collector, is Oscar Handlin's *Harvard Guide to American History* (Harvard University Press, 1966). It is an invaluable guide to the study of every aspect of American history, containing a listing of the great historical libraries which are in most cases open to the public. It also contains a listing of aids for locating books, pamphlets, and bibliographies. Parts three to six list the important books from 1492 to 1952.

Another important book is *A Guide to the Study of the United States of America, Representative Books*

Reflecting the Development of American Life and Thought, prepared under the direction of R.P. Basler by D.H. Mugridge and Blanche P. McCrum, and issued by the General Reference and Bibliography Division of the Library of Congress in 1960.

The best one-volume bibliography for the Americana collector is *U.S. IANA (1650–1950)*, the revised and enlarged edition by an outstanding bookseller, Wright Howes, published in 1962. Mr. Howes does not list prices for his books but uses symbols or value brackets. In his foreword he says that "A book's current price, like that of any other commodity, is the temporary product of prevailing demand, supply, economic conditions, value of the dollar, taste and fashion, a combination of highly variable, unstable and impermanent influences."

The following are the symbols for his value brackets:

"a" books are worth	from $10.00 to $25.00
"aa"	from $25.00 to $100.00
"b"	from $100.00 to $300.00
"c"	from $300.00 to $600.00
"d"	from $600.00 to $1,000.00
"dd"	from $1,000.00 upwards

Mr. Howes foresaw the increase in value in American books and the following is a short list and the difference between current prices and his listings:

Adair, James. *The History of the American Indians.* London, 1775. First edition. Mr. Howes lists this as an "aa" book and notes that the book is the best eighteenth-century English source on the southern tribes. A copy, with title page mounted and mended, brought 220 pounds at auction in England in 1973. A copy in original condition would probably have brought four hundred pounds. Thus, we are at present (1976) speaking not of an "aa" book but of a "d" book.

Adams, John. *A Defense of the Constitutions of Government in the United States.* London, 1787. First edition. Mr. Howes lists this as an "a" book. A soiled copy brought $150.00 at auction in 1973. This "a" book has become at least a "b" book.

Carson, James H. *Early Recollections of the Mines.* With a map. Stockton, 1852. First edition. Mr. Howes states that it is the first book printed in Stockton and lists it as a "c" item. A copy without the map brought $750.00 at auction in 1973. With the map it is worth a thousand dollars or more, thus moving into the "dd" class.

Flint, Timothy. *Journal from the Red River to the Duachitta or Washita, in Louisiana in 1835.* Alexandria, Va., 1835. First edition. Howes "b." At auction in 1973 it brought $500.00, a "c" rating and on the way up.

Hamilton, Alexander. *A Full Vindication of the Measures of Congress, from the Calumnies of Their Enemies.* N.Y. 1774. First edition. Hamilton's first publication, written at the age of seventeen. Howes lists this as a "b" but at auction in 1973 it brought $600.00, and is certainly a "d" book by now.

Lewis, Meriwether, & Clark, William. *History of the Expedition to the Sources of the Missouri and to the Pacific Ocean.* Philadelphia, 1814. Two volumes. First edition in original printed boards. Howes "dd" which is $1,000.00 upwards, but in 1964 a copy brought $5,200.00 at auction and a rebound copy of the same book brought only $450.00 in 1965 (note the difference in price between the original binding and the rebound copy). A copy in original boards brought $10,000.00 at auction in 1973, and the value of the book is still rising.

Maximillian zu Wied-Neuwied, Prince. *Travels in the Interior of North America.* London, Ackerman, 1843–44. One volume of plates in folio (81 colored, and finished by hand), one volume of text in 4to. First edition. Howes "dd." In 1961 it brought one thousand six hundred pounds. In 1965 it brought three thousand pounds, and in 1973 it brought six thousand eight hundred pounds.

As Mr. Howes noted correctly in the foreword to his book, the dollar's value has diminished; so the prices of most items of Americana and first editions have risen in price. Between 1940 and 1945, Peter Decker, a specialist in Americana, issued four catalogs describing almost 7,500 items of Western Americana collected by George W. Soliday. In 1960 these catalogs were reprinted in one volume with an index. The prices in Decker's catalogs were absurdly low in relation to today's market, but these catalogs were issued more than thirty-five years ago when the interest in collecting Americana had just begun.

A great collection of Americana was sold by the Parke-Bernet Galleries between 1966 and 1969. This was the celebrated library of Thomas Winthrop Streeter, the author of the standard bibliography of Texas. This collection, with prices realized, has been cataloged bibliographically in seven volumes, plus an index volume, by Edward J. Lazare. This catalog, like the one issued by Peter Decker, is invaluable because of its bibliographical notes. Although the Streeter collection brought record prices, it is possible that these prices will be surpassed in the near future because the books are becoming scarcer and demand is becoming greater and greater.

Now that I have discussed the collecting of Americana in general and have suggested background reading and the utilization of a few basic bibliographies, let me begin with a short history of the earliest printing in America and then turn to some specific areas. The logical taking-off point would obviously be in collecting early American imprints: those books published in Colonial America which are important to the understanding of every aspect of American printing—newspapers, books, pamphlets, etc.

The first book printed in America was *The Bay Psalm Book* by John Eliot, printed in 1640 by Stephen Daye at Cambridge, Massachusetts. Forty-five years later, William Bradford, the most important of our colonial printers, established the first press in Philadelphia under the auspices of the Quakers. He was often in difficulties with the authorities and in 1692 he printed a pamphlet for George Keith, a Quaker who was in disfavor with the Society of Friends. Bradford was arrested, but on appealing to Governor Benjamin Fletcher, who was at that time Governor of both Pennsylvania and New York, Bradford was appointed by Governor Fletcher to be the Royal Printer of New York, a state where the Quakers had no jurisdiction. Bradford thus had the honor of establishing the first presses in Philadelphia and New York, and also, much later, in the state of New Jersey.

In 1704 *The Boston News Letter*, the first American newspaper, was printed by Bartholomew Green. However, far more important to the future of the American newspaper was the establishment of the principle of freedom of the press. This was the result of the trial of John Peter Zenger, the publisher and printer of *The New York Weekly Journal* which in 1733 published an attack on William Cosby, the Governor of New York. Zenger was arrested and brought to trial in 1735. Ably defended by Andrew Hamilton, he was acquitted.

The name most familiar to us is the name of Benjamin Franklin, the younger brother of

James Franklin. James was the publisher and printer of the *New England Courant* which incurred the wrath of the Boston authorities. He was forbidden to print and publish his newspaper unless the copy was first approved by the secretary of the province. Dissatisfied with this edict, he conceived the idea of turning the printing over to his younger brother, Benjamin, who was his apprentice. Thus, the *New England Courant* of February fourth to the eleventh, 1723, was published with the imprint of Benjamin Franklin.

Benjamin Franklin was a book collector at a very early age, spending almost all the money he earned to buy books. As with most book collectors, he disliked selling any part of his collection; but finding it more and more difficult to work for his brother James, and without the funds to travel from Boston to seek other employment, he was forced to sell some of his books and with the money thus acquired he set sail for New York.

Arriving in New York, he sought employment with William Bradford. Having no opening for him, Bradford suggested that Benjamin seek employment with his son, Andrew, who operated a printing press in Philadelphia. In this, too, Benjamin was unsuccessful. Justifiably, there have been scores of books written on the life of Benjamin Franklin. For my purpose, which is a short history of printing in North America, suffice it to say that after many trials, he set up his own press in Philadelphia in 1728.

The first printed Bible in a European lan-

guage, German, was done by Christopher Sauer
in Germantown, Pennsylvania, in 1743. The second Bible to appear in America, and the first Bible in the English language, was printed by
Robert Aitken in Philadelphia in 1782. Later Bi-
bles printed in the Eastern part of our country
have very little value while those printed west of
the Mississippi in the early 1800s do have.

Besides Benjamin Franklin, William Bradford,
and Samuel Green and his family, the only other
name of great consequence in Colonial printing
was Isaiah Thomas, who was born on January 19,
1749. Thomas died in 1831, but not until he had
written, printed, and published a *History of Printing in America* which was, until 1936, the authoritative book on early printers and printing.
Thomas was the founder and first president of
the American Antiquarian Society in Worcester,
Massachusetts. He gave the Society his extensive
library and, upon his death, most of the fortune
he had acquired. The Society has one of the
finest collections of Americana in the country
and welcomes all who wish to use its resources. In
1936, Douglas McMurtrie projected a four-vol-
ume history of printing in the U.S. Unfortunately, he was able to complete only one volume
which covered the middle and Atlantic states.
This volume was the second volume and the only
one ever published.

In Douglas McMurtrie's *The Book. The Story of
Printing and Bookmaking,* there is a fine chapter
on the spread of printing in America. In fifteen

pages it gives a short but comprehensive account of the printers and the states in which they worked.

To respond to another question—"How old must an American book be to have any value?"—the answer is that age alone has no necessary relation to the value of a book. *The Bay Psalm Book,* which was printed in 1640, is the most valuable of American books, primarily because it was the first book printed in the United States, and not alone because of its age; it is also a great rarity. The first book, pamphlet, broadside, or newspaper printed in any town or city of any state or territory in the United States is valuable because it is the first printing and not because of any intrinsic value of the item, although if the item is important historically, its value is increased. Here follows a short list of the states and the time and place in which their printing began:

1.   STATES AND TERRITORIES WEST OF THE MISSISSIPPI.

   Arizona—The first press was established in Tubac in 1859. Presses were established in Solomonville, Tempe, and Yuma in 1888.

   California—The earliest printing was done in Monterey in 1833 under Mexican auspices, and in 1854 the first printing was done in Grass Valley, Oakland, and Placerville.

   Colorado—The earliest printing was done in Denver and Mountain City in 1859 and in Leadville in 1879.

Idaho—The earliest printing was done in Clear Water in 1839 and Desmet in 1888.

Illinois—Matthew Duncan was the first printer in Illinois and the first product of his press appeared in Kaskaskia in 1814.

Other states west of the Mississippi and first dates of presses are Texas, 1817; Iowa, 1836; Minnesota, 1849; Nevada, 1858; and Utah, 1849. Montana and Wyoming were the last states to have printing (in 1863). Many of these printers, particularly in the West, were itinerant journeymen, traveling from place to place, setting up temporary quarters, and moving on when work ran out. This is the main reason why imprints from the Western States are rare.

2. THE EASTERN STATES.

Connecticut—Earliest printing was done by Thomas Short in New London in 1709. Stonington and Wallingford had their first presses in 1798.

Delaware—Earliest printing was done by James Adams in Wilmington in 1761. Dover had its first press in 1799.

Maryland—In 1685 William Nuthead produced the first printing in St. Mary's City. He died in 1695 and his widow took over the press, the first woman in America to be in complete charge of a printing press. Her role in this enterprise lasted only one year. William Parks opened a printing shop at Annapolis in 1726.

New York, New Jersey, and Pennsylvania,
were, as previously mentioned, three states
whose printing presses were established by
William Bradford:
>   New Jersey—At Perth Amboy in 1723.
>   New York—At New York City in 1693.
>   Pennsylvania—At Philadelphia in 1685.

Since printing was introduced late in the seventeenth and early in the eighteenth century in the Eastern states, imprints after 1776 have little value unless they were the first imprints of a particular city or town.

3. THE NORTHEAST.

Maine—Its first press was established by
Benjamin Titcomb at Falmouth in 1785.
In 1798 a press was begun in Fryeburg.

Massachusetts—The first press in the Continental United States was established by
Stephen Daye (or Day) in 1639, and in
1640 he printed *The Bay Psalm Book*, the
first book printed in America.

New Hampshire—Daniel Fowle opened a
printing shop at Portsmouth in 1756. In
1799 a press was established at Gilmanton.

Vermont—In 1778 Alden Spooner opened a
printing shop. Thirty years later Montpelier had its first press.

Except for Massachusetts, printing in the
Northeast was established immediately before, or

a little after 1776, so books printed within that period have some value.

4. THE SOUTH.

  Alabama—In 1807 an unknown printer established the first press in the state at Wakefield, which was at that time in the Mississippi Territory. Jacksonville and Marion had their first presses in 1838.

  Arkansas—W.E. Woodruff, the first printer in Arkansas, opened a printing shop in 1819. Thirty-five years later a press was introduced in Helena.

  Florida—John Wells and William Charles Wells, the first printers in Florida, issued a newspaper at St. Augustine in 1783. In 1838, St. Joseph had its first press.

  Georgia—James Johnston established the first press in 1763 at Savannah.

  Kentucky—John Bradford established the first press in 1787 at Lexington and the first product of his press was the newspaper *The Kentucky Gazette*.

  Louisiana—Denis Braud founded a press in New Orleans in 1765. Sixty-one years later a press was established at Donaldson.

Besides the dates above for imprints from the Southern states, any book, pamphlet, or broadside printed in the Confederacy during the Civil War has value. That value is predicated on their desirability and scarcity. *In fact, desirability and scarcity are two factors determining the valuation of all first editions of whatever category. The other factor is condition.* Condition is so important that I emphasize—*do not* buy any volume in shabby or, particularly, incomplete state regardless of price, unless the book is very rare in any state.

Comprehensive information on imprints in the United States can be found in the many excellent bibliographies on the subject. The most thorough is the work on imprints in the states of the United States issued by the Works Progress Administration from 1939 to 1942. Your documents or reference librarian can guide you to this very important series. Other important bibliographies on the subject are C.K. Shipton and J.E. Mooney's *National Index of American Imprints Through 1800, The Short-Title Evans,* 2 vols., American Antiquarian Society and Barre Publishers, 1969; G.T. Tanselle's *Guide to the Study of U.S. Imprints,* 2 vols., Cambridge, 1971; and the many imprint inventories written by Douglas C. McMurtrie. Stanley Wemyss in his *The General Guide to Rare Americana,* new enlarged edition, Philadelphia, 1950, lists many scarce and important titles including imprint dates, but it is not as thorough as the other previously listed titles.

To collect Americana in all its phases, the following titles are of the utmost importance. They are the bibliographies that are essential to a complete understanding of the subject; if they are not available for purchase, and many of them are scarce, the majority can be found in any good reference library, college or public:

Adams, Ramon F. *The Rampaging Herd. A Bibliography of Books and Pamphlets on Men and Events in the Cattle Industry.* Univ. of Oklahoma Press (1959). An important bibliography listing 2651 items.

Adams, Ramon F. *Six-Guns and Saddle Leather. A Bibliography of Books and Pamphlets on Western Outlaws and Gunmen.* Univ. of Oklahoma Press (1954). An excellent bibliography.

A.I.I. *Check-list of Chicago Ante-Fire Imprints 1851-71.* Chicago, 1938.

Ayer Collection. *Narratives of Captivity Among the Indians of North America, with Supplement.* 2 vols. Chicago (1912, 1928).

Bradford, T.L. *Bibliographer's Manual.* 5 vols. Philadelphia, 1907–1910.

Bristol, R.P. *Supplement to Charles Evans' American Bibliography.* University of Virginia (1970).

John Carter Brown Library. *Catalogs* (of the Collection). Providence, 1865–71, 1875–82, 1919–31.

Clark, T.D. *Travels in the Old South.* 3 vols. Norman, Okla., 1956–59.

Cole, George W. (Compiler). *A Catalogue of Books Relating to the Discovery and Early History of North and South America, Forming a Part of the Library of E.D. Church from 1482 to 1884.* 5 vols. Illustrated with facsimiles. Peter Smith (reprint) 1951. One of the greatest libraries of Americana.

Cowan, R.E. *A Bibliography of the History of California and the Pacific West 1510–1906.* New edition with an introduction by Henry R. Wagner and additional notes by Robert G. Cowan. Columbus, Ohio, 1952.

Cox, F.G. *A Reference Guide to the Literature of Travel.* 3 vols. Seattle, 1935.

Crandall, M.J. *Confederate Imprints: A Check-list.* 2 vols. Boston, 1955.

Dobie, J.F. *Guide to the Life and Literature of the Southwest.* Dallas, 1952. An honest and outspoken guide, for example:

> HARRIS, FRANK. *My Reminiscences as a Cowboy.* 1930. His comment: "A blatant farrago of lies, included in this list because of its supreme worthlessness."

Another example:

> HAGEDORN, HERMAN. *Roosevelt in the Bad Lands.* Boston, 1921. His comment: "A better book than Roosevelt's own *Ranch Life and the Hunting Trail.*"

Evans, Charles. *American Bibliography.* 12 vols. Issued from 1903 to 1934. Vol. 13 issued in 1955 by C.K. Shipton. In 1960, the New York Public Library issued a checklist of additions to Evans.

Field, T.W. *An Essay Towards an Indian Bibliography. Being a Catalog of Books Relating to the American Indian.* N.Y., 1873.

Gohdes, C. *Bibliographical Guide to the Study of Literature of the U.S.* 3rd edition, revised and enlarged. Duke University Press, n.d.

Guerra, Francisco. *American Medical Bibliography 1639-1783.* N.Y., 1962.

Harwell, R.B. *More Confederate Imprints.* 2 vols. in one. Virginia State Library, 1957.

Hubach, R.R. *Early Midwestern Travel Narratives.* Detroit, 1961.

Hunnewell, J.F. *Bibliography of the Hawaiian Islands.* Detroit 1962.

Jones, Herschel V. *Adventures in Americana 1492–1897.* A selection of books from his Library. 2 vols. N.Y., 1928.

Larned, J.N. *The Literature of American History, a Bibliographical Guide.* Boston, 1902. Reprinted. Columbus, Ohio, 1953.

Matthews, William. *American Diaries: An Annotated Bibliography of American Diaries Written Prior to the Year 1861.* Boston, 1959.

Meisel, Max. *A Bibliography of American Natural History.* 3 vols. Originally published in 1924. Reprint. N.Y., 1967.

Monaghan, Jay. *Lincoln Bibliography 1829–1939.* 2 vols. Springfield, 1943–45.

Nevins, A.; Robertson, K.I., Jr.; and Wiley; B.I. *Civil War Books. A Critical Bibliography.* 2 vols. Baton Rouge (1967, 1969). An essential book for collectors of Civil War material.

Nickles, John M. *Geologic Literature on North America 1785–1918.* Part One—Bibliography. Washington (G.P.O.), 1923.

Peel, B.B. *Bibliography of the Prairie Provinces.* (Toronto, 1956.)

Phillips, P.I. *Atlases in the Library of Congress.* 5 vols. Washington (1909–1958).

Rader, Jessie L. *South of Forty, from the Mississippi to the Rio Grande. A Bibliography.* Norman, Okla., 1947.

Sabin, Joseph; Eames, W.; and Vail, R.W.G. *Dictionary of Books Relating to America from its Discovery to the Present Time.* 29 vols. Issued from 1868 to 1936. Both the Evans and Sabin were done on Micro cards by the Readex Corp. in New York. Each collection is contained in one box. A book is rare indeed if it is not listed in Evans or Sabin.

Smith, C.W. *Pacific Northwest Americana.* 3rd revised edition. Portland, 1950.

Storm, Colton. *A Catalog of the Everett D. Graff Collection of Western Americana.* Chicago, Newberry Library, 1968. Lists 4801 items with full bibliographical descriptions.

Streeter, Thomas W. *Bibliography of Texas 1795-1845.* 5 vols. Cambridge, 1955–60.

Ullom, Judith C. *Folklore of the North American Indians: An Annotated Bibliography.* Library of Congress, Washington, 1969.

Wagner, H.R. *The Plains and the Rockies. A Bibliography of Original Narratives of Travel and Adventures 1800–1865.* Revised and extended by Charles L. Camp. 3rd edition. Columbus, 1953.

Wheat, C.I. *Books of the California Gold Rush.* San Francisco, 1949.

Wheat, C.I. *The Mapping of the West.* 4 vols. San Francisco, 1958–60.

IV
Collecting American Juveniles

The following is an excerpt from an address given by Justin Schiller at the May Massee Symposium on Creative Publishing for Children, at Kansas State Teachers College in 1971. It is reprinted with his kind permission:

First and foremost, anyone interested in maintaining a book collection should try to understand the motivation behind this pursuit. In part, this requires a blanket acceptance in wanting to collect—as opposed to merely accumulating or liking books. There may be some who think of collecting as a form of investment, calculating that an increase in value would be more money than could be made in a savings account during the same period of time. If these people are given wise counsel by a specialist bookseller or collector, then they should achieve their objective; however, it is wrong to compare making a profit with the personal delight of finding some long sought-after volume. The degree of pleasure is quite different. To a serious collector, financial gain certainly carries with it a satisfaction that his own taste and judgment predicted the market or that he had recognized a valuable book and succeeded in buying it for much less than it was worth; but to simply remove or cancel out the sentiment which goes with the mechanical aspects of collecting, then what remains is a very sterile end product despite the sophistication or expertise employed in its means.

A collector must always be aware of the limitations of the reference tools. For example, Dr. Rosenbach's *Early American Children's Books,* published in 1933 (reprinted in 1966), is an annotated listing of a personal library which made no pretense at completeness. In all, 816 volumes are described as published up to the year 1836, but to designate any book as being rare if it is not recorded in so general a collection is a flagrant misuse of a reference bibliography. On the other hand, in the exhaustive study by the late d'alte A. Welchon, *Children's Books in America to 1821* (Worcester, American Antiquarian Society, 1972), there are listed 1300 individual titles of juveniles in all known editions up through 1820—nearly 8000 entries—any nursery book not described in this work would indeed be rare.

The interest in collecting American juveniles has grown tremendously in the last fifteen years, and values have grown with it. The Scribner Book Store was the first shop to do a specialized catalog of children's books in the early 1940s. It listed a very fine copy of L. Frank Baum's *The Wizard of Oz* at $65.00. The standard price today for an average copy of *The Wizard* is probably $600.00 to $950.00, depending on condition.

The Wizard is not the only book that Baum wrote; there are many of his books, however, which bring less than one hundred dollars each. Some of his books were written under the following pseudonyms: Floyd Akers, Laura Bancroft, John Estes Cooke, Capt. Hugh Fitzgerald, Suzanne Metcalf, Schuyler Staunton, and Edith Van Dyne. The books published under the name of Edith Van Dyne are relatively common, the others are scarce. None of them, however, are expensive.

The books of Horatio Alger and Edgar Rice Burroughs have increased in value but are still within reach of a modest purse with the exceptions of the first editions of Alger's *Ragged Dick* and Burroughs *Tarzan of the Apes*. Many of the books cataloged in Jacob Blanck's *Peter Parley to Penrod* can still be bought at less than astronomical figures. In his preface, Blanck writes that his work is an attempt to direct attention to certain books, once popular, that have been all but forgotten or overlooked. There are many modern writers of children's books who are overlooked today, particularly the winners of the Newbery and Caldecott awards from 1922 to the present time. They are collected but are relatively inexpensive.

In this country, we have an abundance of fine illustrators of children's books, many of them bringing high prices. The works of Maxfield Parrish, Howard Pyle, Frederic Remington,

Charles Russell, and N.C. Wyeth have reached record prices recently but rarely in the hundreds; but the work of illustrators such as Pamela Bianco, Wanda Gag, Edmund Gorey, Will James, Dorothy P. Lathrop, Ernest Thompson Seton, Maurice Sendak, Dr. Seuss, and many, many others can still be bought at reasonable prices.

William Targ, who has written delightfully on every aspect of book collecting, has this to say about children's books:

> Collecting children's books is a kind of return to the first euphoric childhood of memory, the recalled world of fantasy and adventure, mirrored in the magic of printer's ink and paper. It is a sentimental journey, if you will, to the best of all possible worlds, that of childhood. And what, after all, is collecting but affectionate appreciation stemming out of early impressions, nostalgia, and new understanding.
>
> A good children's book strikes a vibration in the soul that lasts a lifetime. And when a reader or collector achieves maturity and a special sense of values, he may recognize that the best books are really those that children have loved for many generations of lifetimes.

I do not believe that anything more could possibly be said about the joys of collecting juveniles; so, collect those authors that have delighted you in the past, and may your children also find delight in them.

For collectors of American juveniles here follows a few bibliographies, some of which have been mentioned previously:

Barry, F.V. *A Century of Children's Books*. N.Y. (1923).

Blanck, Jacob. *Peter Parley to Penrod, A Bibliographical Description of the Best-Loved American Juvenile Books*. Cambridge, 1961.

Bolton, Theodore. *American Book Illustrators*. Bibliographic checklists of 123 artists. N.Y., 1938. Valuable for the juvenile collector as well as for the collector of illustrated books.

Davidson, Gustav. *First Editions in American Juveniles and Problems in their Identification*. Chicago, Normandie House (1939).

Gottlieb, Gerald. *A Descriptive Catalog of an Exhibition* (of children's books) *at the Pierpont Morgan Library*. Pierpont Morgan Library, N.Y., 1975. A useful and important reference work.

Johannsen, Albert. *The House of Beadle and Adams and its Dime and Nickel Novels*. 2 vols. Norman, Okla., 1950.

Kerlan, Irvin. *Newbery and Caldecott Awards. A Bibliography of First Editions*. Minneapolis, 1949.

Kiefer, Monica. *American Children Through Their Books 1700–1835*. Philadelphia, 1948.

Kingman, Lee, ed. *Newbery and Caldecott Medal Books: 1956–1965*. Boston, 1965. These awards are given each year by the Children's Services Division and the American Association of School Libraries of the American Library Association. The Newbery Award is given for the most distinguished contribution to American literature for children; the Caldecott Award for the most distinguished American picture book for children.

Meigs, Cornelia, & Others, eds. *A Critical History of Children's Literature. A Survey of Children's Books in English from Earliest Times to the Present.* N.Y. (1953)

Miller, B.H., & Field, E.W., eds. *Newbery Medal Books: 1922–1955.* Volume two: *Caldecott Medal Books: 1938–1957.* 2 vols. Boston (1965–66).

Rosenbach, A.S.W. *Early American Children's Books, with Bibliographical Descriptions of the Books in his Private Library.* Foreword by A.E. Newton, N.Y., 1966.

Sloane, William. *Children's Books in England and America to the Seventeenth Century. A History and Check-list.* N.Y., 1955.

Targ, William, ed. *Bibliophile in the Nursery. A Bookman's Treasury of Collector's Lore on Old and Rare Children's Books.* Cleveland (1957). My favorite, and a book I never tire of reading, finding new and useful information each time.

Toronto Public Library. *The Osborne Collection of Early Children's Books. 1476 to 1910.* 2 vols. Toronto Public Library. Volume one published previously; volume two in 1975. An excellent catalog containing 5300 entries, American and European.

Welchon, d'alte A. *Children's Books in America to 1821.* Worcester, American Antiquarian Society (1972).

The collecting of children's books has grown to such proportions that complete auction sales have been given over entirely to juvenilia, and with great success.

V
Collecting Private Press Books and Fine Typography

Charles J. Sawyer and F.J. Harvey Darton in *English Books 1475–1900, a Signpost for Collectors,* 2 vols. Westminster, 1927, have written:

> The best definition of a private press is that it is an enterprise, conceived, and masterfully and thoroughly carried out, by a creative artist who (whether or not he likes to cover some of his expenses by sales) does his work from a sincere conviction that he is expressing his own personality.

Will Ransom, the foremost historian on private presses and their work, refers to the productions of the private presses as the typographic expression of a personal ideal conceived in freedom and maintained in independence. His reasons for using the expression "conceived in freedom" was that during the infancy of printing, and particularly in England during the fifteenth and sixteenth centuries, private presses were used in attacks on the Church, on Kings, and on local authorities. The press was often moved from place to place in wagons to escape detection.

The private press, whose function was to produce beautiful books, began in England with the establishment of the Strawberry Hill Press in 1757 by Horace Walpole; but it was in the nineteenth century that the English private presses became famous all over the world. The Daniel Press, The Vale Press, The Ashendene Press, the Doves Press, The Essex House Press, the Kelmscott Press, and many others had a tremendous impact on American private and commercial presses.

William Morris has written that he began printing books with the hope of producing some which would have a definite claim to beauty, at the same time being easy to read but not dazzling to the eye or troubling to a sense of proportion by eccentricity of form in the letter types selected.

The Kelmscott Press of William Morris has produced beautiful books, but critics contend that the purpose of a printed book is to be read and not solely as an object of admiration. His books are difficult to read because the mind is distracted by the masses of decoration on every page.

The impact of the Kelmscott Press on America is described by Douglas McMurtrie in this way:

Morris speedily gained many enthusiastic admirers who imitated his typographical style with great zeal but little taste. Few, indeed, are the type-specimen books issued in the United States during the late

90's which do not contain an ugly, blotchy, black type with some fantastic ornaments intended to accompany it. These found a ready market among printers who supplied themselves with some thick paper and a quantity of red ink and set out to do artistic printing, but succeeded only in perpetrating inconceivable typographical monstrosities.

Clark Conwell was strongly influenced by the work of the Kelmscott Press, but he was no imitator of William Morris. At his Elston Press in New Rochelle, New York, he produced *The Vision of William Concerning Piers the Plowman* in 1901 which resembles the Kelmscott *Chaucer,* but by 1904 he produced Longus' *Daphnis and Chloe* which, while resembling some of Morris's productions, shows some degree of typographic independence.

During the early years of the twentieth century, many private presses were established in different parts of the United States and conflict arose as to whether printing was an art form. Beatrice Warde claimed that printing could not be classified as a work of art since its main function was to convey ideas. It may please the eye, but it must transfer thoughts, ideas, and images from the mind of the writer to the mind of the reader. Edwin Grabhorn agreed with that dictum since he has written that:

> Printing in its childhood was an art. . .because childhood moves by spontaneous inner urge, not by rules and intellectual bondage that run into fixed

molds. . .but the art of printing became a science, then a craft. . .and finally a trade.

The great type designers in America were men to whom typography as an art was intended only for one purpose—to create a page that would please the eye but would not interfere with the message the author intended to convey.

It seems to me, however, that both Beatrice Warde and Edwin Grabhorn overstate the case when they write that printing is no longer an art, as when the latter says that "Printing was aimed at suitability, the scholar and critic displaced the master craftsman, and the advertising artist was added by way of variety."

The types created by Frederic W. Goudy, Rudolph Ruzicka, D.W. Dwiggins, Bruce Rogers, Frederic Warde, and scores of others certainly disprove their contention that type design is not an art form. They have proved that a page can still be beautiful and exceptionally readable.

The productions of our American private presses and the typographical work done by our master craftsmen for trade publications are not nearly as expensive as books from the Doves Press, the Kelmscott Press, the Ashendene Press, and other private presses in England; but I believe that a great deal of the work produced by our typographers and type designers is equal to many of the English efforts.

Those interested in collecting examples from private presses and books designed by our great typographers should read and study Will Ransom's *Private Presses and Their Books*, N.Y., 1929. The following is a short list of my choices of a few of the more important printers and private presses taken from Ransom's book.

Elmer Adler. The Pynson Printers, Inc. Founded in 1923.

Peter Beilenson and S.W. Wallach. The Peter Pauper Press. Founded in 1927. This is now a commercial press, but still printing charming books.

Will H. Bradley. The Wayside Press. Founded in the 1890s.

Clark Conwell. The Elston Press. Founded in 1900.

Theodore Low De Vinne. Printer and scholar who printed many books for the Grolier Club and was the author of many books on typography.

Richard W. Ellis. The Georgian Press. Founded in 1927.

Frederic W. Goudy and Bertha M. Goudy. The Village Press. Founded in 1903.

Edwin and Robert Grabhorn. The Grabhorn Press. Founded in 1919.

Thomas Bird Mosher. The Mosher Books. Founded in 1891.

Bruce Rogers. One of the most important figures in modern fine printing. Designer of books for the Riverside Press from 1903 to 1912, typographic designer to Harvard University Press,

and designer of books for William Edwin
Rudge. His Lectern Bible is one of the greatest
productions of any press in America.
Carl Purington Rollins. The Montague Press.
Founded in 1911. Later the printer and de-
signer for the Yale University Press.
William Edwin Rudge. Printer and publisher.
Ralph Fletcher Seymour. The Alderbrink Press.
Founded in 1897.
Daniel Berkeley Updike. The Merrymount
Press. Founded in 1893. The author of the
authoritative book on printing, *Printing Types,
Their History, Forms, and Use.* 2 vols. 3rd edi-
tion, Cambridge, 1962. A type designer of
note, whose books at present do not bring the
prices they deserve.
Frederic Warde. Designer of books, principally
for W.E. Rudge.
George Parker Winship. The Sign of the George.
Founded in 1920.

There are many other private presses, printers, and designers of type that are worth collecting, including the early volumes of the Limited
Editions Club, many of them designed by D.B.
Updike, John Henry Nash, Frederic W. Goudy,
Edwin and Robert Grabhorn, and the Lakeside
Press of Chicago. Choose the ones that please
you; but *condition is of the utmost importance* in collecting private press books. As I have stressed
previously, condition is important in collecting
books of all categories, but it is particularly so in

press books. For additional study I recommend the following:

Bennett, Paul A., ed. *Books and Printing. A Treasury for Typophiles.* Cleveland (1951).

Cockerel, Douglas. *Bookbinding and the Care of Books.* 5th edition. N.Y. (1953).

The Colophon, a Quarterly for Bookmen. Any of the four series issued are worth reading and studying. They date from 1930 to 1950.

The Dolphin, a Journal of the Making of Books. Numbers one and two issued by the Limited Editions Club in 1933 and 1935.

McMurtrie, Douglas C. *The Book. The Story of Printing and Bookmaking.* N.Y., 1937.

McMurtrie, Douglas C. *Type Design: An Essay on American type design with Specimens of the Outstanding Types.* Introduction by Frederic W. Goudy. Pelham, N.Y., 1927.

For the impecunious collector I suggest the Heritage Press Books (which are reprints of the Limited Editions Club) and the limited editions published by Thomas Bird Mosher. Mosher's books are eminently readable, many of them small enough to fit in pocket or purse.

VI
Collecting American Sporting Books

The Olympic Games were the earliest organized sport activities, probably begun in 776 B.C. and continuing every four years until the fourth century A.D. when they were discontinued by the Emperor Theodosius I of Rome. They were renewed in Athens in 1896 and the first Olympic Games held in the United States were in St. Louis in 1904.

Sport is one of the major activities in America at the present time and its rise in popularity began a hundred years ago. In Colonial times, the Puritans of Massachusetts placed a ban on any and all types of amusement; but in 1618 James the First, King of England, sanctioned a book called *The Book of Sports*. This was an attempt to gain favor with the people of England and the Colonies in the New World by permitting them to enjoy all types of sports. This sanction of a book they found to be obnoxious and abominable so angered the authorities of Massachusetts that they ordered all copies to be burned by the common hangman.

The Puritans of New England had great influence, and as late as 1774 the Continental Congress called for the discouragement of every kind of extravagance, which included all the sports of the day and all entertainments of any kind. However, the Puritan influence did not extend to Virginia, New York, and Pennsylvania. In Virginia, horse racing was the major sport of the pre- and post-Revolutionary period; but this sport, like all sports of the times, was exclusively for gentlemen. In 1732, anglers in Philadelphia founded the Fishing Company of the State in Schuylkill and Philadelphia thus became the first city in the Colonies to have a club devoted entirely to sport.

Gentlemen, and some gentlewomen, were the only citizens who participated in sports; but the end of the Civil War brought a change in this situation. Between 1865 and 1875 nearly seven million immigrants from Ireland and Germany came to this country. The potato famine in Ireland in 1848 had brought many Irish families to this country, but the greatest number came in the post-Civil War period. The majority of them had little or no education, but they brought with them a love of physical activity and a desire to participate in active sports.

They were working men and women and they met with hostility and prejudice; but by the late 1870s they overcame all resistance and sport was open to everyone—everyone that is, except the Negro. Jackie Robinson broke the color line in baseball in October, 1945, when he was hired by Branch Rickey to play for the Montreal Royals, a Brooklyn farm club. In 1947, he was brought up to play for the Brooklyn Dodgers. It took nearly seventy years for Negroes to play with white players in baseball, and many more years were to pass before Negroes were accepted in other sports.

The history of sport in America is shrouded in mystery. We know very little of the origins of our major sports. We do know that basketball was invented in 1891 by A. Naismith; but doubt still exists regarding the invention of baseball. Although the Baseball Hall of Fame is in Cooperstown, New York, the town in which Abner Doubleday supposedly invented the game, many people claim that the game was developed by a group of merchants in New York City who played baseball in an empty lot sometime in 1842. They formed a genteel baseball club called the Knickerbockers in 1845, and they played other teams of gentlemen for the love of the game. Baseball became very popular, and by 1850 it was called The National Game. Nineteen years later, the first professional ball club, the "Cincinnati Red Stockings," was organized and the game was on its way to its great years with Babe Ruth and the New York Yankees of the 1920s.

Bicycles, which are more popular today than

ever before, possibly because of the fear of auto-mobile pollution, were first brought to this coun-try from Europe early in the 1870s. They did not gain wide acceptance until an efficient model was exhibited at the Philadelphia Centennial in 1876.

The first intercollegiate football game was played between Rutgers and Princeton in 1869 at New Brunswick, New Jersey. In 1873 a conven-tion was held at which Columbia, Princeton, Rutgers, and Yale were represented. A set of rules was adopted, and the foundation was laid for intercollegiate matches. The first post-sea-son Rose Bowl game was played in 1902, and it has been conducted annually since 1916.

Organized professional clubs, begun in 1920, formed the American Professional Football As-sociation with a roster of ten clubs. Intercolle-giate games were more popular and attracted greater crowds. Today the tide has turned, with professional football out-drawing the college games.

Professional sports which followed were hock-ey and golf; with soccer and tennis suddenly be-coming large spectator sports in the last few years. The American public who were for so long merely spectators have become participants and the golf courses, tennis courts, and ski trails are overcrowded, with hours of waiting time for each activity.

Did the W.P.A. foresee this trend in 1938, or was it only to create jobs that they built 10,000 tennis courts, 3026 athletic fields, 2261 horseshoe courts, 1817 handball courts, 805 swimming pools, 318 ski trails, and 254 golf courses? The demand for these recreational facilities has increased tremendously since that time, and, with the shortened work week, sport may become the most important industry in the United States.

Collecting American sporting books, particularly of those sports from which you derive the greatest amount of pleasure, is not an expensive hobby if you can resist the early books on the subject or editions limited to a few copies. But of course if you collect seriously you will eventually want these as well. Following is a list of bibliographies and some other important books which are mainly historical and may help you in your decision of selection:

Derrydale Press. *A Decade of American Sporting Books and Prints 1927-1937*. A complete bibliography of the books and prints published. N.Y., 1937. All the books published by this press were limited editions and some are quite expensive.

Dulles, F.R. *America Learns to Play. A History of Popular Recreation 1607–1940*. With a bibliography. N.Y., 1940.

Gee, E.R. *Early American Sporting Books*. The Derrydale Press, 1929.

Hallock, C. *The Sportsman's Gazeteer and General Guide to the Game Animals, Birds, and Fishes of North America*. N.Y., 1883. Contains a bibliography.

Henderson, R.W. *Early American Sport.* A checklist of books by American and foreign authors published in America prior to 1860. Second, revised and enlarged edition. N.Y., 1953. It contains 1217 editions of 628 titles.

Higginson, A.H. *British and American Sporting Authors.* Bibliography by S.R. Smith. Berryville, Va., 1949.

Madow, Pauline, ed. *Recreation in America.* With a bibliography. N.Y. 1965.

Phillips, J.C. *A Bibliography of American Sporting Books.* Boston (1930).

The books that follow, although not bibliographies, should be of additional help in your choice of subject:

Ballou, M.M. *Sportsman's Portfolio of American Field Sports.* 1855. Reprint—The Derrydale Press, 1929.

Boyle, R.H. *Sport—Mirror of American Life.* Boston (1963).

Cozens, F.W. *Sports in American Life.* Chicago (1953).

Durant, J. *Pictorial History of American Sports from Colonial Times to the Present.* Revised edition, N.Y. (1965).

Gee, E.R. *The Sportsman's Library.* Being a Descriptive List of the Most Important Books on Sport. N.Y., 1940. Includes foreign authors.

Henderson, E.B. *The Negro in Sports.* Washington (1939).

Herbert, Henry William, an Englishman who migrated to America in the 1830s, was the first writer in America to earn a living by writing sporting books. This he did under the name of Frank Forester. Under that name he wrote *Field Sports of the United States* and *Fish and Fishing of the United States* in 1849, and he later wrote other books on sporting activities. He wrote nonsporting novels under his own name but they were not nearly as popular as his sporting books.

Holliman, J. *American Sports (1785–1835)*. Durham, North Carolina, 1931.

Manchester, H.H. *Four Centuries of Sport in America 1490–1890*. N.Y. The Derrydale Press, Reprint—N.Y. (1968).

Phillips, J.C. *Classics of the American Shooting Field 1783–1926*. Edited by J.C. Phillips and L.W. Hill. Boston, 1930.

As an example of a rare and expensive book, the *Sportsman's Companion, or, an Essay on Shooting*, N.Y., 1783, is the first book on sport printed in America and is attributed to Charles Bell.

VII
Collecting Detective, Mystery, Fantasy, and Science Fiction

The birth of the detective story in English began in the United States with the writings of Edgar Allan Poe in 1841. Mystery stories, puzzle stories, and crime stories had existed for hundreds of years. The Chinese were particularly fond of mystery and puzzle stories, as were the Greeks and Hebrews; but until Poe wrote and published *The Murders in The Rue Morgue* no one had written a detective story.

Until the nineteenth century the fictional detective had not appeared in print, mainly because he did not, in fact, exist in real life. The apprehending of a suspected criminal was haphazard at best. No Nero Wolfe, Sam Spade, or Sherlock Holmes tracked down the culprit by virtue of sifting evidence, seeking motives, and assembling sets of circumstances and clues, and in the denouement triumphantly naming and nabbing the real criminal. Arresting a suspected criminal was, for the most part, in the hands of the military, or civic vigilante groups, who made no serious attempt to prove guilt, but rather picked up a likely suspect simply on the basis of his being accused, disreputable, or disliked in the community. The reader of the "crime" book of the period did not enjoy the fun and challenge of guessing who had done it, but got his kicks rather in the trial and ultimate punishment of the victim, usually by torture or public hanging.

As London and Paris grew in size and population, the need arose for some other system to combat the rise in crime. Early in the 1800s, London formed the Bow Street Runners—which later became Scotland Yard. Paris developed the Surete, its own criminal department, and its most renowned member was Francois Eugene Vidocq, whose autobiography was published in 1829. These developments paved the way for the entry on the literary scene of the fictional detective.

There seems to be no doubt that Poe had read Vidocq's *Autobiography* and was influenced by it. He admired everything French and was admired in return. He used Paris as the background for his detective stories, and his detective, C. August Dupin, is the most important fictional detective in all literature. (Sherlock Holmes is not included because he was not a detective, but a "private eye.")

Poe wrote three detective stories, all three having Dupin as the central figure. The first story was *The Murders in The Rue Morgue,* which first appeared in *Graham's Magazine* for April,

1841. Poe was then editor of the magazine. Its second appearance was in the pamphlet *Prose Romances #1,* published in 1843. Its price was twelve and a half cents. A copy in original wrappers would today be worth over a hundred thousand dollars. The second detective story was *The Mystery of Marie Roget,* based on a real crime. This appeared in Snowden's *The Ladies' Companion* in the issues of November and December, 1842, and February, 1843. The third story, *The Purloined Letter,* was published in *The Gift* for 1845, a collection of poetry, prose, and engravings by various authors and artists, usually published once a year. All three stories plus *The Gold Bug* were published in 1845 as *Tales.* Thus *Tales* was the first book of detective stories in the English language by an American.

After Poe, the most important American writer of detective stories was Anna Katherine Green. Her classic, *The Leavenworth Case,* was published in 1878 and its main character was police detective Ebenezer Gryce. After Green came Jacques Futrelle, who was born in 1875 and died in the sinking of the Titanic in 1912. He wrote two important books, the first being *The Thinking Machine: Being a True and Complete Statement of Several Intricate Mysteries Which Came Under the Observation of Professor Augustus S.F.X. Van Dusen,* N.Y., 1907, reissued in 1929 as *The Problem of Cell Thirteen.* The other book was *The Thinking Machine on the Case,* N.Y., 1908. After Futrelle, there followed such writers as Raymond

Chandler, Dashiell Hammett, Melville Davisson Post, Ellery Queen, Rex Stout, S.S. Van Dyne, and scores of others.

Collecting first editions of American detective fiction offers a myriad of delights. Not only are you involved in the intricacies of the author's plots, but you also collect the main ingredients of the writer's imagination, his hero—the detective. The detective-hero may be connected with the police or he may be working on his own as a "private eye." Fictional detectives come in all shapes, sizes, and temperaments: the suave, urbane Nick Charles (Hammett); the obese gourmand whose passion is growing orchids, Nero Wolfe (Rex Stout); the inscrutable Charlie Chan (Biggers); the tough Continental Op (Hammett); the earthy Philip Marlowe (Chandler); etc. These are just a very few of my favorites. Collect yours and enjoy the chase, and the delights of finding that elusive book.

So much for the detective story. The mystery novel is something else again. The important element in a mystery story is the element of suspense which can be produced behind the scene and which the reader cannot see or be aware of. At the finish, the components fall into place with sleight-of-hand dexterity.

In his *Murder for Pleasure*, which is the finest book written on the history of the detective story, Howard Haycraft defines the difference between the detective and mystery in this way:

The dividing line between the physical type of detective story and the pure mystery is often difficult to distinguish. The conclusive test might well be whether, in the final analysis, the solution is accomplished by incident (mystery story) or deduction (detective story). Even by this test, it is not easy to decide in which of these categories the dramatic and highly popular murder stories of Mary Roberts Rinehart belong. They fall almost exactly on the border line.

I have read both detective fiction and mystery stories extensively. My enjoyment comes principally from the detective story and Haycraft's definition is an exceedingly good one.

The history of science fiction and fantasy literature dates back almost two thousand years, the first publication being Lucian of Samosata's *Icaromenippus,* written in the second century A.D. and describing a voyage to the moon. The second publication was Johannes Kepler's *Somnium,* written in Latin and published in 1634. Kepler had studied the work of Nicolaus Copernicus and Galileo and had been associated with Tycho Brahe. Thus his book was the first book of science fiction written with a knowledge of science.

The first story of a trip to the moon written in English was Bishop Francis Godwin's *The Man in the Moone,* which was published in 1638. Many stories of voyages to the moon were published in the next two hundred years, the most famous being Cyrano de Bergerac's *Voyages to The Moon and The Sun,* which appeared in an English translation in 1659.

In 1818, Captain John Cleves Symmes claimed that the earth was hollow and consisted of five concentric spheres empty at the poles and each habitable. With the collaboration of James McBride he published his *Theory of Concentric Spheres* in 1826. There had previously appeared a science fiction story, *Symzonia* (1820), published under the pseudonym of Captain Adam Seaborn.

The theories of Captain Symmes influenced many writers, the most famous being Edgar Rice Burroughs, who wrote six inner-world novels—*At the Earth's Core, Pellucidar, Tanar of Pellucidar, Tarzan at the Earth's Core, Back to the Stone Age,* and *Land of Terror.* Besides the inner-world novels, Burroughs wrote ten Martian novels and four Venus novels. Burroughs died in 1950 but is still the most widely read of all science fiction writers.

Among the many writers who are still read today and are important to the development of science fiction are Fitz-James O'Brien, whose *The Diamond Lens* was published in 1858; Ignatius Donnelly, who wrote three science fiction novels; and L. Sprague de Camp, who has written many. The most important perhaps was Hugo Gernsback, who wrote *Ralph 124C 41 Plus: A Romance of the Year 2660.* His importance stems not from his book but from his publishing *Amazing Stories,* the first magazine devoted exclusively to science fiction. The first issue appeared in April, 1926, and with its popularity assured, other magazines followed in rapid succession—*Science Wonder Stories, Air Wonder Stories, Astounding Stories of Super Science,* and many, many others.

There is still divided opinion as to the difference between science fiction and fantasy. In many instances they overlap but are not congruent. John W. Campbell, an important figure in the development of science fiction, distinguishes them by saying that a story is science fiction if the writer believes it could happen, fantasy if he thinks it could not. Fletcher Pratt believes that any story with a scientific background should be classed as science fiction and not fantasy, but he admits it is not a good definition. His criticism of most science fiction is that there is a lack of minor detail; the characters seem to float in space and live on air, they never eat a meal, go to bed, or relax with the space-time equivalent of a book. For this reason, fantasy has the edge on science fiction since both the events and surroundings are impossible from the beginning.

The Gnome Press in New York, the Shasta Press in Chicago, and the Fantasy Press in Reading, Pennsylvania, publishers of fantasy and science fiction, are out of business and have been for many years. The one remaining—and the most important of them all—is Arkham House and its two subsidiaries: Mycroft and Moran and Stanton & Lee. Arkham House was founded by August Derleth and Donald Wandrei in 1938, and their first book was H.P. Lovecraft's *The Outsider and Others*. It was published in 1939 in an edition of 1268 copies and is a very difficult book to find. The press has consistently published books of great merit in the fantasy field and is continuing to do so. Their list of in-print authors is impressive, including Ray Bradbury, August Derleth, Robert E. Howard, H.P. Lovecraft, Clark Ashton Smith, Donald Wandrei, and many others.

The first comprehensive bibliography of fantastic literature was *The Checklist of Fantastic Literature, a Bibliography of Fantasy, Weird, and Science Fiction Published in the English Language*, by Everett F. Bleiler, Chicago, 1948. It has drawbacks, since it is difficult to determine whether a title listed is a first edition, first issue, or first state; it is an important milestone, however, and reasonably complete to 1948.

Some other books besides Bleiler's that are important to an understanding of the subjects covered in this chapter, and which include bibliographies, are the following:

Bailey, J.D. *Pilgrims Through Space and Time. Trends and Patterns in Scientific and Utopian Fiction.* N.Y. (1947).
Barzun, J., and Taylor, W.H. *Catalogue of Crime. Being a Reader's Guide to the Literature of Mystery, Detection, and Related Genres,* N.Y., 1971.
Bretnor, R., ed. *Modern Science Fiction, Its Meaning and Its Future.* N.Y. (1953).

Carter, John, ed. *Detective Fiction: A Collection of First and a Few Early Editions.* A catalog issued by the Scribner Book Store in 1934. The collector who bought from that catalog had the wisdom and imagination to foresee the tremendous interest in the genre, and the unbelievable increase in price.

Clareson, T. *Science Fiction Criticism, an Annotated Checklist.* Kent State University Press (1972).

Dade, T.M., compiler. *The Annals of Murder. A Bibliography of Books and Pamphlets on American Murders from Colonial Times to 1900.* Norman, Okla., 1961.

De Camp, L. Sprague. *Science–Fiction Handbook. The Writing of Imaginative Fiction.* N.Y., 1953.

Hagen, D.A. *Who Done It? An Encyclopedic Guide to Detective, Mystery, and Suspense Fiction.* N.Y., 1969.

Haycraft, Howard, ed. *The Art of the Mystery Story.* A Collection of Critical Essays, edited and with a commentary by Haycraft. New edition, indexed. N.Y., 1976.

Haycraft, Howard. *Murder for Pleasure, the Life and Times of the Detective Story.* Newly enlarged edition. N.Y., 1972. A must for any aficionado of the genre.

Hubin, Allen J., Editor. *The Armchair Detective.* A Quarterly Journal Devoted to the Appreciation of Mystery, Detective, and Suspense Fiction. An excellent fan magazine, with articles and bibliographies by writers in the field.

Address for subscription: "The Armchair

Detective", 243 12th St. Drawer P, Del Mar, Ca. 92014. Subscription price is $10.00 per year.

MacGowen, K., ed. *Sleuths: Twenty-three Great Detectives of Fiction and their Best Stories.* N.Y. (1931). Valuable for the accounts of detectives preceding each story. Both English and American authors are covered.

Penzoldt, Peter. *The Supernatural in Fiction.* (London, 1952).

Pratt, Fletcher, ed. *World of Wonder, an Introduction to Imaginative Literature.* N.Y. (1951).

Queen, Ellery. *The Detective Short Story. A Bibliography.* New introduction. Although published in 1942, this is still the most important bibliography on the subject. N.Y., 1969.

In the Queen's Parlor, and other Leaves from the Editor's Notebook. N.Y., 1969.

Queen's Quorum. A History of the Detective–Crime Short Story as Revealed in the 106 Most Important Books published in this Field since 1845. Supplements through 1967. N.Y., 1969.

Thomson, H.D. *Masters of Mystery: A Study of the Detective Story.* (London, 1931.)

Wollheim, Donald A. *The Universe Makers, Science Fiction Today.* N.Y. (1971).

Detective stories are most in demand by collectors; with fantasy, science–fiction, and mystery stories following in that order.

VIII
Collecting Illustrated Books

There is a very close kinship between the artists who illustrated juveniles and those who illustrated other books than juveniles. Many of our best artists illustrated books for both children and adults, including Valenti Angelo, Peggy Bacon, Cyrus Le Roy Baldridge, Paul Bransom, Paul Brown, Charles Livingston Bull, Lynd Ward, Rockwell Kent, N.C. Wyeth, and many others.

Many artists were more than mere illustrators: they were painters whose work commands attention, and whose paintings hang in museums throughout the country. Many of them were interpreters of the old West and the American Indian. Artists like George Catlin, Will James, Tom Lea, William Robinson Leigh, Frederic Remington, Charles M. Russell, Ross Santee, John W. Thomason, and others are represented. First editions of books which include one or more illustrations by famous artists are often enhanced, or even made valuable, by the illustrations.

Very few of us can afford to buy the elephant

folio edition of Audubon's *Birds of America,* which was published in England. Even if we could afford the price, a copy with all 435 plates intact is almost impossible to find. It took Audubon eleven years to complete the set. He worked on it from 1827 to 1838. It appeared without letter-press, and the text was finally published in Great Britain in five volumes during the years 1831 to 1839.

The first American edition was in octavo, published in seven volumes with the full five hundred plates and the text from the English edition. It was issued in one hundred parts with printed paper wrappers or bound in half or full morocco. The plates for this edition were reen-graved under the supervision of Audubon. It was published in New York and Philadelphia from 1841 to 1844. This set has also become quite expensive. In 1937, Macmillan of New York issued a one-volume edition which was quite good, and in recent years many editions in brilliant color have appeared on the market.

The interest in collecting color plate books of American natural history, flowers, birds, etc., has increased to an extent that the important books are not within reach of the average purse. For instance, two books by William P.C. Barton—one on the flora of North America in three volumes with 136 hand-colored engravings issued in Philadelphia from 1821 to 1823 and the same author's *Vegetable Materia Medica of the United States; or, Medical Botany, etc.,* illustrated with fifty exqui-sitely colored engravings made after original drawings from nature by the author, 2 vols., Philadelphia, 1817–1818—are almost impossible to find at any price.

Books with hand-colored engravings have not been published for many years, but new techniques have produced many beautiful color-plate books in the last twenty-five years, and many can be bought at reasonable prices.

The Limited Editions Club has used the talents of many fine artists to illustrate its books, and with the exception of the books by Matisse and Picasso, most of them can be purchased for less than fifty dollars each, some for a little more than a hundred. Here are some of the fine books it has produced:

Aesop. *Fables*. Illustrations redrawn from Florentine woodcuts by Bruce Rogers. Oxford University Press, 1933.

Benet, S.V. *John Brown's Body*. Illustrations in color by John Steuart Curry. London, 1948.

Book of Psalms, The. Illustrated and Illuminated by hand by Valenti Angelo. Mt. Vernon, 1961.

Dickens, C. *A Christmas Carol*. Hand-colored illustrations by Gordon Ross. Boston, 1934.

Dreiser, T. *An American Tragedy*. Illustrated by Reginald Marsh, his final work. N.Y., 1954.

Leonard, Wm. E. Translation of *Beowulf*. Lithographs in color by Lynd Ward. N.Y., 1952.

Lewis, S. *Main Street*. Illustrated by Grant Wood. Chicago, 1937.

London, J. *The Call of the Wild.* Illustrated by Henry Varnum Poor. Los Angeles, 1960.

Maugham, W.S. *Of Human Bondage.* Etchings by John Sloan. 2 vols. Yale University Press, 1938.

Stephens, J. *The Crock of Gold.* Illustrated by Robert Lawson. N.Y., 1942.

Whitman, W. *Leaves of Grass.* Photographic illustrations by Edward Weston. 2 vols. N.Y., 1942.

Wilde, O. *The Ballad of Reading Gaol.* Lithographs by Zhenya Gay. N.Y., 1937.

Each of the Limited Editions Club books was printed by an important press here or abroad; each was signed by the artist. This is but a small sampling of the five hundred books it has published and continues to publish.

Some other famous American artists who illustrated books which are collected are as follows: George W. Bellows, Thomas H. Benton, A.B. Frost, William J. Glackens, Gordon Grant, Winslow Homer, E.W. Kemble, Thomas Nast, Maxfield Parrish, Joseph Pennell, Howard Pyle, Rudolph Ruzicka, and Grant Wood.

There are literally scores of American artists whose books you might like to collect. I repeat, collect those that please you, and may you enjoy the search. The following may be of some help in your hunt for illustrated books:

Bennett, Whitman. *A Practical Guide to American Nineteenth Century Color Plate Books.* N.Y., 1949.

Bolton, Theodore. *American Book Illustrators. Bibliographic Checklists of One Hundred and Twenty-three Artists.* N.Y., 1938.

Stauffer, D. McNeely. *American Engravers on Copper and Steel, with Mantle Fielding's Supplement.* 3 vols. Philadelphia, 1917.

Taft, R. *Artists and Illustrators of the Old West.* N.Y., 1953.

Along with visiting bookstores, reading their catalogs, and watching the auction sales, I strongly recommend to the collector, beginner or sophisticated, a subscription to *AB Bookman's Weekly.*

While this is an indispensable tool for booksellers, it is filled with invaluable information for everyone interested in antiquarian books, whether they be librarians, dealers, or private collectors. Each issue is filled with articles by leading authorities concerning happenings in the book world, bibliographical book reviews, notices of forthcoming auction sales, exhibitions, and book fairs, with detailed reports on the fairs. Trends in auction prices are discussed with up-to-the-minute reports of prices or high spots.

The main body of the journal consists of columns of "Books Wanted" advertisements from dealers and libraries (the only ones permitted to use the columns). These columns provide an outlet for a duplicate item you may have, or a book you no longer have interest in. There are also "books for sale" advertisements and possibly that elusive book for which you have been searching may crop up in this section, often at a reasonable price.

Specialist dealers offer to buy and sell books on a variety of subjects and many offer catalogs or specialty price guides for nominal sums.

AB was founded and, until recently, edited and published by Sol Malkin, now retired. At present it is under the able editorship of Jacob L. Chernofsky, with Mary Ann O'Brian as book review editor. Subscriptions can be secured by writing to: Antiquarian Bookman, Box 1100, Newark, N.J. 07101.

I urge you to subscribe. You will find it most rewarding.

IX
Buying First Editions
and Americana at Auction
and from Dealers

The first advertised auction sale in America was held in Boston in 1713. From 1713 to 1829, many auction houses flourished and then disappeared from the scene. In 1829, Bangs & Co. began operating an auction gallery in New York City. They stayed in business continuously until they sold the company to John Anderson. The Anderson Galleries became the Parke-Bernet Galleries, which was purchased a few years ago by Sotheby's of London. The gallery is now known as Sotheby Parke Bernet Inc.

For the beginner, the buying of books at auction is a hazardous undertaking. You are not only competing against experts who know the value of the book in question, but you are also bidding against book dealers who consider the buying of books at auction as part of their livelihood. They are either buying for stock or for a client at a commission. Buying for yourself is pitting your knowledge against that of a more experienced foe. Until you have gained the requisite knowledge about the values of the books you are collecting, I would suggest that you commission a dealer to buy for you and pay him his commission, usually ten percent plus travel expenses. You will find that you have made a friend and an adviser and saved money as well, despite the commission. If you do attend a sale, determine in advance the maximum amount you wish to pay for any given item and stick to your guns. Auction sales can be exciting and educational and sometimes surprisingly profitable. It's a great feeling to have a book which you planned to bid up to $50.00 knocked down to you for considerably less. It could, and does, happen.

The following is a list of the major auction houses in America:

California Book Auction Galleries. 224–28 McAllister Street, San Francisco, CA 94102. They conduct twelve sales a year, and the cost of the catalogs is $15.00 plus $10.00 for their price lists (optional).
Christie's. 867 Madison Avenue, New York, NY 10021. One-year subscription to catalogs costs $100.00.
Samuel T. Freeman & Co. 1808–10 Chestnut Street, Philadelphia, PA 19103. Catalogs on request.

Harris Auction Galleries. 873 N. Howard Street, Baltimore, MD 21201. Six or more sales each year. The cost of catalogs with prices realized is $14.00.

Montreal Book Auctions, Ltd. 1529 Sherbrooke St. West, Montreal, P.Q. H3G 1L7, Canada. They hold at least twelve sales yearly and the cost of their catalogs and price lists is $24.00.

Sotheby Parke Bernet Inc. 980 Madison Avenue, New York, NY 10022. One-year subscription to catalogs, including pre-sale estimates and post-sale prices, costs $30.00.

Swann Galleries, Inc. 104 E. 25th Street, New York, NY 10010. They hold about forty sales a year, and catalogs and price lists cost $60.00.

I suggest that you subscribe to the Sotheby Parke Bernet and the Swann Galleries catalogs, since although they are expensive in relation to the cost of the catalogs from the other auction houses, they are well worth the price. They, as well as some of the other houses, will accept your order bids if you are unable to attend the sale. They are two of the best auction houses, and their price lists are valuable; these lists appear at least a year before the publication of *American Book Prices Current (ABPC)*.

American Book Prices Current is issued yearly. It is more than a mere listing of prices realized at auction in America and Europe—it often gives bibliographical information of great value to a collector. It has major drawbacks, however, in that it does not list the condition of a book unless it is a poor copy or a very fine copy. Most of the books sold at auction fall between these two categories. Other factors that contribute to the price at auction are demand and rarity. Another determining factor, an important one, is the number of people bidding for the same book. One can readily see that if three or more people are bidding for an item, the price will usually be higher than if one or two are bidding. This competitive fact cannot be determined by reading one year's prices. My advice is to check *ABPC* for a period of five years or more, since only in that way can you determine whether the books that interest you are rising or falling in value.

There is a fascination about the antiquarian bookstore that cannot be described. I have tried to express this quality for almost fifty years, and without success. Christopher Morley, among many others, has tried to describe this fascination in his *The Haunted Bookshop*, and he came closest to realizing it. You must visit the shops yourself, and perhaps you will discover what I mean.

In urban areas there are probably many antiquarian dealers who would welcome your visit. In these shops you can look around to your heart's content, and if you are careful in handling their wares, you will not be disturbed. Most dealers in secondhand and rare books are free with their knowledge, and may help you in locating books, and will sometimes even suggest other shops where a likelihood exists that the book you are searching for can be found.

People who live in small towns should use the *American Book Trade Directory, 1975–76,* published by R.R. Bowker Co., 1180 Avenue of the Americas, New York, N.Y. 10036. It lists booksellers by state and city, noting whether or not they are antiquarian dealers and listing their specialties. If they are antiquarian, write for their catalogs. If you can't get to dealers throughout the country, let *them* bring their shelves to you through their catalogs. It's worth it. If possible, buy from a catalog even though an item may cost slightly more than your estimated value. You will then remain on mailing lists. Catalogs are becoming very expensive to produce and dealers are reluctant to maintain large mailing lists of people who collect catalogs and nothing else.

Just a few of the many dealers worth visiting or contacting are as follows (a preliminary phone inquiry might be advisable):

Black Sun Books. 667 Madison Avenue, New York, NY 10021.
Specialty—Modern First Editions and Rare Books.
The Arthur H. Clark Company. 1264 South Central Avenue, Glendale, California. Specialty—Americana.
Dawson's Book Shop. 535 N. Larchmont Blvd., Los Angeles, CA 90004.
Specialty—Western Americana, Books About Books, Rare Books.

Dragon Press. Elizabethtown, NY 12932. Specialty—Fantasy and Science Fiction.

Duschnes, Philip C. 699 Madison Avenue, New York, NY 10021. Specialty—First Editions, Limited Edition Club publications.

Goodspeed's Book Shop. 18 Beacon Street, Boston, MA 02108.

Heritage Book Shop. 6707 Hollywood Blvd., Hollywood, CA 90028.
Specialty—Modern First Editions, Fine Printing, Rare Books.

The Holmes Book Co. 274 Fourteenth Street, Oakland, CA 94612.
Specialty—Western Americana.

John Howell–Books. 434 Post Street, San Francisco, CA 94102.
Specialty—Americana, First Editions, Press Books.

The Jenkins Company. Box 2085, Austin, TX 78767.
Specialty—Western Americana, Literary First Editions.

Kaleidoscope Books. P.O. Box 108, Watertown, MA 02172.
Specialty—Detective Stories, Fantasy, and Science Fiction.

Edward Morrill & Son, Inc. 25 Kingston Street, Boston, MA 02111.
Specialty—Americana.

Kenneth Nebenzahl, Inc.   333 North Michigan Ave., Chicago, IL 60601.
Specialty—Western Americana, Literary First Editions.

Justin G. Schiller, Ltd. 36 E. 61st Street, New York, NY 10022.
Specialty—Children's Books, Bibliography, the Graphic Arts.

Seven Gables Bookshop, Inc. 3 W. 46th St., New York, NY 10036.
Specialty—American Drama, Fiction and Poetry, Children's Books.

University Place Bookshop. 821 Broadway, New York, NY 10003.
Specialty—The Negro.

Fred White, Jr. Box 3698, Bryan, TX 77801.
Specialty—Western Americana.

Whitlock Farms—Books. Sperry Road, Bethany, CT 06525.
Specialty—Americana, Children's Books.

Ximenes Rare Books. 120 E. 85th St., New York, NY 10028.
Specialty—Rare English and American First Editions.

And last, but not least:

Biblo & Tannen Booksellers & Publishers, Inc. 63 Fourth Ave., New York, NY 10003.
Specialty—Americana, First Editions, Detective Fiction, and General Literature.

X
Recommended Books for Additional Reading and Study, and Summation

These are the books I recommend for your consideration and enjoyment:

Altick, Richard D. *The Scholar Adventurers.* N.Y., 1951.

Altrocchi, Rudolph. *Sleuthing in the Stacks.* Cambridge, 1944. Includes a long scholarly chapter on the ancestors of Tarzan.

American Women. *A Selected Bibliography of Basic Sources of Current Historic Interest.* Dept. of Labor, Women's Bureau. Washington, 1950.

Arnold, William H. *Ventures in Book Collecting.* N.Y., 1923.

Bookmen's Holiday. Notes and Studies Written and Gathered in Tribute to Henry Miller Lydenberg. N.Y., 1943.

Brewer, Reginald. *The Delightful Diversion: The Whys and Wherefores of Book Collecting.* N.Y., 1935.

Browne, A. *The One Hundred Best Books by American Women During the Last Hundred Years*. Chicago, 1933.

Burke, W.J.,& Howe, W.D. *American Authors and Their Books 1640 to The Present Day*. Augmented and revised by I.R. Weiss, N.Y., 1962.

Carter, John. *ABC for Book Collectors* New Revised edition. N.Y. 1963.

————*Books and Book Collectors*. Cleveland and New York (1957).

————*New Paths in Book-Collecting*. London, 1934.

————*Taste and Technique in Book-Collecting*. N.Y., 1948.

These four books by John Carter are an absolute must for anyone interested in collecting first editions.

Coan, O.W., & Lillard, R.G. *America in Fiction, an Annotated List of Novels that Interpret Aspects of Life in the U.S., Canada and Mexico*. 5th edition. Pacific Books, Palo Alto, Ca., 1967.

Curle, R. *Collecting First editions; Its Pitfalls and Its Pleasures*. Indianapolis (1930).

Currie, Barton. *Fishers of Books*. Boston, 1931.

De Ricci, S. *The Book Collector's Guide: A Practical Handbook of British and American Bibliography*. Philadelphia, 1921.

Dictionary Catalog of the Schomburg Collection of Negro Literature and History in the New York Public Library. Boston, 1962. One of the best collections in the United States.

DuBois, W.E.B. *A Select Bibliography of the American Negro.* 3rd edition. Atlanta, 1905.

DuBois, W.E.B., & Johnson, G.B. *Encyclopedia of the Negro.* Preparatory Volume with Historical Reports. N.Y., 1946.

Flexner, Eleanor. *Century of Struggle, the Woman's Rights Movement in the U.S.* Cambridge, 1959.

Franklin, M.L. *The Case for Woman Suffrage. A Bibliography.* N.Y., 1913.

Grolier Club. *One Hundred American Influential Books Printed Before 1900.* Grolier Club, 1947.

Hart, James D. *The Oxford Companion to American Literature.* 4th edition, revised and enlarged. N.Y., 1965.

Hazard, Paul. *Books, Children & Men.* Translated by Marguerite Mitchell. Boston (1966).

Jackson, Holbrook. *The Anatomy of Bibliomania.* 2 vols. in one. N.Y., 1932.

Jackson, Holbrook, compiler. *Bookman's Pleasure. A recreation for booklovers.* N.Y., 1947.

Jameson, J.F. *The History of Historical Writing in America.* N.Y., 1961.

Jordan-Smith, Paul. *For the Love of Books.* The Adventures of an Impecunious Collector. N.Y., 1934.

Leonard, A., Drinker, S.H., and Holden, N.Y. *The American Women in Colonial and Revolutionary Times 1565–1800.* A Syllabus with Bibliography. Philadelphia (1962).

MacLeod, Anne S. *A Moral Tale: Children's Fiction and American 1820–1860.* Hamden, Conn, 1975.

Muir, P.H. *Book-Collecting as a Hobby*. N.Y., 1947.

Newton, A.E. *The Amenities of Book-Collecting and Kindred Affections*. Boston, n.d.

Newton, A.E. *This Book-Collecting Game*. Boston, 1928.

Orcutt, William D. *From my Library Walls*. N.Y. (1945).

Oswald, J.C. *Printing in the Americas*. N.Y., 1937.

Parrington, Vernon L. *Main Currents in American Thought*. Three volumes in one. N.Y. (1930).

Pearson, Edmund L. *Books in Black or Red*. N.Y., 1923.

Powell, Lawrence C. *Books in my Baggage. Adventures in Reading and Collecting*. Cleveland and New York (1960).

Powell, Lawrence C. *A Passion for Books*. London (1959).

Randall, David A. *Dukedom Large Enough*. (Reminiscences of a Rare Book Dealer 1929–1956.) N.Y. (1969).

Rosenbach, A.S.W. *A Book Hunter's Holiday. Adventures with Books and Manuscripts*. Boston (1936).

Rosenbach, A.S.W. *Books and Bidders. The Adventures of a Bibliophile*. Boston, 1927.

Ross, F.A., and Kennedy, L.V. *A Bibliography of Negro Migration*. N.Y., 1934.

Slater, J.H. *The Romance of Book-Collecting*. N.Y., 1898.

Starrett, Vincent. *Bookman's Holiday. The Private Satisfactions of an Incurable Collector*. N.Y. (1942).

Starrett, Vincent. *Books Alive. A Profane Chronicle of Literary Endeavor and Literary Misdemeanor.* N.Y.,1940.

Storm, C., and Peckham, H. *Invitation to Book Collecting. Its Pleasures and Practices.* N.Y., 1947.

Targ, William, ed., with introduction and notes. *Bouillabaisse for Bibliophiles.* Cleveland and N.Y. (1955).

Targ, William, ed. *Carrousel for Bibliophiles. A Treasury of Tales, Narratives, Songs, Epigrams, and Sundry Curious Studies Relating to a Noble Theme.* N.Y., 1947.

Thompson, Ralph. *American Literary Annuals and Gift Books 1825-1865.* N.Y., 1936.

Winsor, J. *Narrative and Critical History of America.* 8 vols. Boston, 1889.

Winterich, J., and Randall, David A. *A Primer of Book Collecting.* N.Y., 1966.

Wolf, 2nd., E., with J.F. Fleming. *Rosenbach. A Biography.* Cleveland, (1960).

Work, M.N. *A Bibliography of the Negro in Africa and America.* N.Y., 1928.

Now that you have gone through this book, the time has come to re-emphasize the two main reasons why it was written and to renew what the author hopes you have gleaned from it. The first and foremost reason is to help you in the identification of first editions by American publishers. The second is to provide a listing of some of the tools, the bibliographies, you will require to enable you to continue to build your library and better enjoy the world behind the making of it.

I cannot stress too forcefully the importance of collecting FIRST EDITIONS. This is the most challenging and the most rewarding aspect of collecting. You will have learned by now that identifying first editions is not really an exact science. It is hoped, however, that sufficient information has been given to enable you to recognize the firsts of most major publishers. For those books where you are not sure, you will know which bibliographies to consult.

WHAT TO COLLECT has been gone into only in general terms. The major fields have been covered, but there are an infinite number of specialized areas open to suggestion. To list all of them would require a volume many times the size of this one. A few further suggestions follow:

Books on all aspects of American transportation are available, affordable, and collectable. These include the stagecoach, canal barges, the automobile, trolley cars, railroads, and others.

From Christopher Columbus, through John Paul Jones, to Admiral Dewey, and on to the modern navigators, thousands of fine books have been written on American history through its oceans and inland waterways. If you are a landlubber, through your books you can paddle an Indian canoe through American streams, command a *Monitor* or a *Merrimac,* pilot a clipper ship out of New England, navigate the Mississippi in a paddle-wheeler, be exhilarated by your imagination, and in the end—have a wonderful collection.

The possibilities for collecting the different

phases of Americana are limitless. The following are challenging if you want to try for completeness, but are not expensive: a complete set of the Lakeside Classics issued once a year by the Lakeside Press, with each book a reprint of an American classic. A complete set in first editions of the W.P.A. Guides to the States. A complete set in first editions of the Rivers of America. A complete run of the charming Valentine's Manuals of the City of New York with reproductions, many in color, of streets, houses, parks, etc.

The collecting of books on women in America and the impact they have had on our culture is a recent trend and offers many opportunities for the adventurous collector.

Books on and by the Negro have been collected for many years, yet there are many books to be found to round out a good collection. This requires patience but the results can be very rewarding.

The charming gift books issued in the 1830s, '40s, and '50s are hard to find in very good condition, but worth the effort. Besides the engravings which adorn all such books, they contain valuable first editions of many important authors of the period.

The first editions of our philosophers, scientists, sociologists, historians, and economists are collected but not to any great extent. Bargains can still be found in these fields, and a good collection can be made without too great an outlay of money.

Finally, here is a suggestion for off-beat collecting. A former customer of mine, the late Dr. Judson Gilbert, collected Literary Doctors of Medicine. In his lifetime, Dr. Gilbert collected first editions by medical doctors who wrote books on literature and the humanities. For example: S. Weir Mitchell, an American physician, wrote (among other books) *Hugh Wynne, Free Quaker,* an important American novel, in 1898. This kind of collecting opens up great vistas for the collector. How about statesmen, lawyers, engineers, and so forth, who wrote books on subjects far afield from their professions?

So pick your field, sally forth to your local bookseller, buy your first book, and unless I am greatly mistaken, you will be hooked on the great addiction—bibliomania.

Index

140 INDEX

REFERENCE